KU-497-333

The NO-NONSENSE GUIDE to

HUMAN RIGHTS

Olivia Ball and Paul Gready

The No-Nonsense Guide to Human Rights
First published in the UK in 2006 by
New Internationalist™ Publications Ltd
Oxford OX4 1BW, UK
www.newint.org
New Internationalist is a registered trade mark.

Cover image: Bunia prison, Democratic Republic of Congo.
Mark Renders/Getty Images

Series editor: Troth Wells
Design by New Internationalist Publications Ltd.

 Printed on recycled paper by T J International Limited, Cornwall, UK
who hold environmental accreditation ISO 14001.

British Library Cataloguing-in-Publication Data.
A catalogue record for this book is available from the British Library.

Library of Congress Cataloguing-in-Publication Data.
A catalogue for this book is available from the Library of Congress.

ISBN 10: 1-904456-45-6
ISBN 13: 978-1904456-452

Foreword

IN ONE WAY or another human rights have been an ever-present reality in my life.

South Africa has been at the forefront of the human rights imagination for the best and worst reasons. Under apartheid the country was an international pariah, spurned and boycotted. Now it has emerged into the embrace of freedom and the international community, with a Constitution that is the envy of the world. I have been so richly blessed to serve as a loudhailer about injustice, when many others were silenced during the 1980s, and to help to usher in the new dispensation as the Chairperson of the Truth and Reconciliation Commission (TRC).

Of course, everything is not perfect. I keep making myself a bit unpopular by saying so! Too many people in South Africa live in poverty and without hope. Inequalities are stark. But enormous progress has been made and South Africa is an inspiration to people across the globe.

Ours is a remarkable story. I have heard many remarkable stories. I recall a young man blinded by police gunfire coming to tell his story to the TRC. When he had finished his testimony, one of the panel asked how he felt after relating his experience. He smiled and though still blind said, 'You have given me back my eyes'. Telling his story was therapeutic and helped to rehabilitate his dignity and selfworth. What he had undergone was not a futile thing. It had contributed to the birth of the new South Africa.

This book is about another remarkable story: the relatively short, yet hugely powerful, emergence of the modern human rights movement. Our struggle in South Africa was all about, and is still about, human rights. For respecting human rights means respecting that every person is unique and is entitled to a life of dignity and choice.

Foreword

Such a message knows no boundaries or limits. It is neither unique to nor forbidden by any culture, religion or political creed. It is as relevant to the current so-called 'war on terror' as it is to individual countries or communities fragmented by conflict or poverty. That it is as urgently necessary now as it ever has been goes without saying.

In South Africa there is much talk about the 'unfinished business' of the TRC. Human rights too is a project with much 'unfinished business'. I commend to you *The No-Nonsense Guide to Human Rights* as a call to question, to think, to act, and to contribute.

The Most Reverend Desmond M Tutu
Anglican Archbishop Emeritus of Cape Town
1984 Nobel Peace Prize Laureate

CONTENTS

Introduction

DURING THE COURSE of writing this book, Olivia spent a lot of time sitting at a bedside in an intensive care unit. Advanced technologies and specialist nursing saved her newborn baby from certain death. The incredible luck of living near a world-class pediatric hospital that never sent a bill for what must have cost the government a small fortune did not escape her. Set in a global context, the luck of many of us living in developed countries is mind-boggling. What part of that is a right – the birthright of all humanity – and what part is just a bonus?

At around the same time, Paul was conducting research in Rwanda and South Africa. In the former, he was moved by people's struggles with the aftermath of genocide. Many activists and organizations were engaged in difficult balancing acts: working with the current government, which some regard as 'strong' and others 'authoritarian', but also trying to influence decision making. Activists may frown at the former, while the government often resists the latter. In pursuit of justice, past and present, both are necessary.

In South Africa Paul visited a local NGO responding to the killing of three young men – boys really – by police during the apartheid era. Funded to construct a public memorial, the NGO questioned why those it would honor lay in unmarked graves. And so it raised more money – mainly from the lawyers who had represented both perpetrators and victims – and now three gravestones accompany the memorial to the dead. Such struggles for dignity lie at the heart of what human rights are about.

'Doing' human rights traverses the mundane and dramatic. It is close to home, as well as in far away places. It requires creativity and courage. But it is not always serious and difficult – human rights work is often fun, sometimes hilarious, and time and again involves forging the most extraordinary friendships.

We hope in this book to illustrate the many entry-points to this evolving endeavor. We cover the history and ideas behind human rights and the laws, institutions and political struggles that strive to uphold them. You will gain insight into the experience of rights violation and the views of those dedicating their lives to rights protection. Moreover, we show how human rights apply to real life, whether in the sterile glare of an operating theater, or in acts of remembrance. We hope in this respect to have made it an 'owner's manual'. Human rights is an exciting, unfinished project of immense potential. You can be part of it.

Olivia Ball
Melbourne

Paul Gready
London

Acronyms used in this book

ANC African National Congress (South Africa)
AU African Union
CAT Convention Against Torture and other Cruel, Inhuman or Degrading Treatment or Punishment
CEDAW Convention on the Elimination of All Forms of Discrimination Against Women
CERD Convention on the Elimination of All Forms of Racial Discrimination
CESCR Committee on Economic, Social and Cultural Rights
CRC Convention on the Rights of the Child
DRC Democratic Republic of Congo
EU European Union
FBI Federal Bureau of Investigation (USA)
FGM female genital mutilation
IACHR Inter-American Court of Human Rights
ICC International Criminal Court
ICCPR International Covenant on Civil and Political Rights
ICESCR International Covenant on Economic, Social and Cultural Rights
ICJ International Commission of Jurists
ICRC International Committee of the Red Cross
ICRMW International Convention on the Protection of the Rights of All Migrant Workers and Members of their Families

ICTR International Criminal Tribunal for Rwanda
ICTY International Criminal Tribunal for former Yugoslavia
IDP internally displaced person
IGO inter-governmental organization
IHL international humanitarian law
ILO International Labour Organization
IMF International Monetary Fund
INGO international non-governmental organization
IRA Irish Republican Army (Northern Ireland)
NGO non-governmental organization
NHRI national human rights institution
OAS Organization of American States
OAU Organization of African Unity
PM Prime Minister
POW prisoner of war
R2P responsibility to protect
RUF Revolutionary United Front (Sierra Leone)
UDHR Universal Declaration of Human Rights
UN United Nations
UN GA UN General Assembly
UNESCO UN Educational, Scientific and Cultural Organization
UNHCR UN High Commission for Refugees
WHO World Health Organization
WTO World Trade Organization

1 A powerful idea

Human rights hold profoundly radical potential, by contesting power and asserting the equality and dignity of every last person. What are they and where do they come from?

MS B, A SECRETARY at an insurance firm in West Africa, agreed to help a friend cater for a party. She had no idea it was a political gathering. The party was raided by police and soldiers and what followed was a nightmare of detention and torture familiar to any reader of Amnesty appeals.[1] Innocent kitchen-hand or unrepentant terrorist, torture is something most of us recognize as a gross violation of rights. But human rights are about much more than political prisoners.

We could begin by saying that they are what's written in international treaties (see box). But human rights represent valid universal claims, regardless of whether they are recognized in law. A comparatively young and incomplete enterprise, human rights is an 'interdisciplinary concept *par excellence*'[2]; a meeting point of anthropology, sociology, economics, philosophy, theology, politics and psychology, as well as law. The law or the state do not grant human rights, they recognize (or trample on) inherent entitlements. In this critical sense, human rights are inalienable from human beings, and exist even in the darkest places of experience where they are most profoundly violated. The revolutionary thing about human rights is that they are for everyone equally, not merely the powerful or virtuous. Oppressed people throughout the world instinctively warm to the idea that human rights are inherent to all humans, precisely because they are human.

Origins of rights

The modern human rights movement originates in World War Two. The closest it has to a founding document is

A powerful idea

What are our rights?

- freedom from discrimination on the basis of birth, race, sex, religion, etc.
- right to life, liberty and security of person
- freedom from slavery
- freedom from torture and other cruel, inhuman or degrading treatment or punishment
- right to personhood and equality before the law
- right to effective remedy for rights violations
- freedom from arbitrary arrest, detention or exile
- right to a fair and public trial
- right to be presumed innocent until proven guilty
- freedom from prosecution for something that wasn't a crime when you did it, and from a heavier sentence than the penalty applicable at the time
- right to privacy
- freedom of movement and residence
- right to leave any country and to return to your country
- right to seek and enjoy asylum from persecution
- right to a nationality
- right to marry and found a family; to protection of the family; to equality in marriage and divorce; freedom from forced marriage
- right to own property and not be arbitrarily deprived of it
- freedom of thought, conscience and religion
- freedom of opinion and expression; right to seek, receive and impart information and ideas through any medium and regardless of frontiers
- freedom of peaceful assembly and association

the 1948 *Universal Declaration of Human Rights* (UDHR). That the United Nations (UN) could in 1945 pledge in its Charter to '*reaffirm* faith in fundamental human rights,' points to ancient traditions of rights (by other names). Most religious texts proclaim altruistic, universal norms of behavior, reflected in the secular human rights credo: 'All human beings... should act towards one another in a spirit of brotherhood (sic).'[3] The absence of a single 'great narrative' of human rights is a strength, allowing us all to participate, from diverse religions, cultures and philosophical traditions.

Two main stories can be told about the genesis of human rights. Neither alone is sufficient but in

- right to take part in government, directly or through freely chosen representatives; to periodic, genuine and secret elections by universal and equal suffrage; to equal access to public service employment
- right to social security in the event of unemployment, sickness, disability, widowhood, old age, etc.
- right to work, to free choice of employment, to just and favorable conditions of work and remuneration, equal pay for equal work
- right to form and join trade unions
- right to rest and leisure, including reasonable limitation of working hours and paid holidays
- right to food, clothing, housing and medical care
- right to special care and assistance for mothers and children
- right to education, including free and compulsory primary education and equal access to higher education
- right to human rights education and peace education
- right to participate in the cultural life of the community, enjoy the arts and share in scientific advancement and its benefits
- right to intellectual property
- right to an international order in which all human rights can be fully realized
- everyone has duties to the community

from the *Universal Declaration of Human Rights*, binding on every country in the world
Note that there are additional, widely recognized human rights found elsewhere, such as those of women and children.

combination they approach a satisfactory account. The first is one of cultural or religious consensus: there is a moral core, even 'rights-like' concepts, in all cultures and religions. This version requires, however, a selective, optimistic reading of all cultures and religions, and can appear somewhat uncritical and static in its understanding of culture. Given that cultures and religions are dynamic, interactive and heterogeneous, the real question is whether human rights can be inserted into, and support, existing moral narratives and processes of change.

The second story is what we call an 'historical evolution' account. It has the promise of progress and

A powerful idea

a happy ending. It can be used, however, to suggest an intersection between particular (often Western) forms of human rights, democracy, market economics, and more – towards which all should evolve and aspire.

Taking the best of both approaches enables human rights to assert the importance of moral progress and change, while applauding diverse histories and acceptable endpoints. Moral progress will require critique of *all* cultures and religions, building on the strengths of *all* cultures and religions. None has a history without blemish, while all have something to offer the rest of humanity. We therefore arrive at a multi-vocal narrative that is both critical and constructive, combining 'what is' with 'what might be', to which everyone can contribute.

The 'consensus' narrative

Antecedents to human rights are found in all cultures and religions. The Ten Commandments given to Moses in the Torah – a basis of Jewish, Christian and Muslim ethics – express the right to life and property in terms of duties, as in 'Thou shalt not kill'. The tradition of synagogues and churches providing asylum also originates in Jewish law.[4] The right to rest can be traced to the Judeo-Christian tradition of *Shabbat* (Sabbath), which also contains a kernel of environmental and economic rights: every seven years agricultural land is to lie fallow, with the poor entitled to gather any yield.

Ancient Hindu law (*Manu Smriti*) contains 10 freedoms and virtues (which the Buddha would later endorse), including freedom from violence, want, exploitation, early death and disease, and fear. Virtues extolled were tolerance, compassion, knowledge and freedom of conscience. The central Buddhist value of nonviolence gives rise to respect for the autonomy of the individual and opposition to coercion.[5]

In East Asia, Confucianism promotes mass education, including moral education. The moral individual courageously pursues what is right, even if doing so is unpopular. Rulers' powers are not unlimited; they are understood as having obligations towards the people, including making 'pulse and grain as abundant as water and fire' and refraining from harsh punishments.[6]

The Qur'an recognizes basic economic rights such as the right to food and housing and protection against poverty, and it exhorts all Muslims to alleviate suffering and need.[7] The advent of Islam in the 7th century was an advance in women's and children's rights in the Arab world. Some feminist scholars argue that the spirit of the Qur'an favors equality between men and women.[8]

The concept of *ubuntu*, found in different forms in east, central and southern Africa, is a cultural world-view of what it means to be human. This Bantu expression is usually translated as 'a human is a human because of other human beings'. In post-apartheid South Africa the term has taken on a political and legal life. It was used to garner indigenous support for the Truth and Reconciliation Commission's work[9] and has appeared in decisions of the South African Constitutional Court.

This brief tour of some religious and cultural

contributions to human rights is, as foreshadowed, a positive, selective reading in support of human rights. This could be a good thing, or a misleading distortion. Culture can be used to 'sell' human rights-related causes, while rights, in turn, can be made to serve nation-building or religious agendas. Are rights-like concepts really like rights or something different? *Ubuntu*, for instance, may add a necessary relational dimension to human rights, but can the relationships it describes still be based on inequality? Areas of cross-cultural consensus do not provide all the answers, but they do suggest 'entry points' linking human rights and diverse religions and cultures, where a conversation can begin. This narrative also shows how different and dynamic cultures and religions can make different contributions over time, thereby linking culture and history.

The 'historical evolution' narrative

The idea that rulers may exercise absolute or arbitrary power has had to be contested throughout the world (again linking the consensus and historical evolution narratives), in order for human rights to take root. The rule of law, fundamental to the protection of human rights, can be traced back to the 18th century BCE. King Hammurabi of Babylonia and Mesopotamia attempted to systematize and publicize the laws of his realm. Hammurabi's Code was an important departure from arbitrary rule.

Christian doctrine would for centuries assert that kings were divinely appointed, but, unlike the

'If the civilizations and ethical contributions of China, India and the Muslim World towered over those of medieval Europe, it is equally true that the legacy of the European Enlightenment, for our current understanding of rights, supersedes other influences.' ∎
MR Ishay, *The History of Human Rights: From Ancient Times to the Globalization Era* (University of California Press 2004) p 7.

Chinese 'Mandate of Heaven', they held absolute power regardless of competence, and were answerable to no-one (but God). Magna Carta, the 'Great Charter' of 1215, subjected the English monarch to the rule of law for the first time. It was violated numerous times during the medieval period, but it was also reissued numerous times, forming irrefutable precedents regarding limits on sovereign power. Italian theologian Thomas Aquinas (1225-74) further opened Christian thinking to the possibility of human rights by maintaining that an unjust king could be overthrown.

Another important development in the history of human rights and accountable government involves two concepts: natural rights and a social contract. Ancient Greek philosophers believed in a universal human nature despite varying human laws and customs. An examination of our nature should suggest 'natural' laws. 'Positive' or enacted law ought to reflect natural law. Rights theorists differ, however, on what is and isn't natural, essential and moral, and for this reason others reject natural law theory.

Swiss-French philosopher Jean-Jacques Rousseau typified the Enlightenment, the major intellectual movement of 18th-century Europe. He hypothesized a 'state of nature' in which our species might have existed prior to the creation of society and government. Complete freedom and equality between all humans was the natural state of things. Democratic government and political rights spring from equality, when we reject the idea that any person or group is born to rule.

We may have enjoyed equality and freedom in the 'state of nature,' but it was also a difficult and dangerous way to live. Writing in an era of emerging nation-states, Rousseau went on to posit a hypothetical 'contract', arising between a group of free, autonomous individuals who agree for the sake of the common good to form institutions of government among themselves. For his predecessor, English philosopher Thomas Hobbes, the contract was between the people and their ruler or government. For the social contract theorist the purpose of government is to secure rights; failure in this regard justifies rebellion.

When writing the *American Declaration of Independence* in 1776, Thomas Jefferson (later President) borrowed extensively from Englishman John Locke, also a social contract theorist: 'Governments instituted among men deriving their just power from the consent of the governed,' and so on. Similarly, Emmanuel Sieyès drafted the French *Declaration of the Rights of Man and Citizen* in 1789 in terms of natural rights and the duty of government to protect those rights.

This 'first human rights revolution' – both radical intellectual movement and transatlantic political revolt – inspired revolutions elsewhere but fell short of the 'true meaning of its creed'. The French Republic, for example, refused to abolish slavery in its colonies or give women the vote. Women's rights advocate Olympe de Gouges was silenced with the blade of a guillotine. Her contemporary across the Channel, Mary Wollstonecraft, also tried to inject sexual equality into the first human rights revolution.[10] In the following generation former slave Sojourner Truth worked to get the rights of black women on the liberal agenda in the US. Disagreements over rights from this era persist today.

In the 19th century it was mainly socialists who carried the movement forward. Industrialization widened disparities of wealth, while limited political access sparked popular revolt. Marx and Engels led a critique of the Enlightenment view of rights; how meaningful are freedoms in a context of economic inequality? Can a capitalist state ever secure rights? They questioned the limitation of suffrage, property rights in general and the 18th-century assertion (still heard today) that free trade advances human

> 'Even though we face the difficulties of today and tomorrow, I still have a dream. It is a dream that is deeply rooted in the American dream. I have a dream that one day this nation will rise up and live out the true meaning of its creed: "We hold these truths to be self-evident, that all men are created equal".' ■
>
> Revd Dr Martin Luther King Jnr, 1963.

rights. Early socialists fought for labor rights, child welfare, the right to education and, contrary to the perception that political rights were an exclusively liberal concern, universal or at least manhood (adult male) suffrage. Despite great opposition, these struggles achieved significant gains, at least in industrialized countries. Parallel rights movements in the 19th century for women's and children's rights and the emancipation of serfs and slaves had both socialist and non-socialist elements. The widespread abolition of slavery was perhaps the greatest rights achievement of that century.

Human rights were never more widely accepted or grossly violated than in the 20th century. At least three genocides were committed: against Armenians, Jews and Tutsis (among others). The two most destructive wars in history were fought, and the worst-ever famine created (China, 1958-61). However, most colonies achieved liberation, women's rights gained unprecedented recognition and the welfare state was born. The latter half of the century was notable for an incomparable worldwide effort to further human rights. But a lesson of history is that progress is never linear, guaranteed or controlled by one part of the world.

Certain lines of critique have accompanied both the 'consensus' and 'evolution' narratives. Contemporary debates often address a convergence of the two themes. We look at two common debates here, examining objections from feminists and, more extensively, cultural relativists.

A powerful idea

From abolition to rendition: a cautionary tale

'The history of torture in western Europe may be traced from the Greeks, through the Romans, through the Middle Ages, down to the legal reforms of the 18th century and the abolition of torture in criminal legal procedure virtually throughout western Europe by the last quarter of the 19th century. Removed from ordinary criminal law, however, torture was re-instituted in many parts of Europe and in its colonial empires from the late 19th century on, and its course was greatly accelerated by changing concepts of political crime during the 20th century. The best recent evidence indicates that torture is used, formally or informally, in one country out of every three.'

If further evidence were needed of the failure of 'historical evolution' to ensure consistent progress in every human right, when President George W Bush declared war on terrorism after 11 September 2001, the US practice of extraordinary rendition – sending suspects abroad to be tortured – expanded 'beyond recognition'. ∎

E Peters, *Torture* (University of Pennsylvania Press 1996) p 5;
J Mayer, 'Outsourcing torture: The secret history of America's "extraordinary rendition" program,' *The New Yorker*, 14 February 2005).

Feminist critiques

Some feminists maintain that human rights, though presented as universal, reflect a masculine perspective. What is male is taken as the basis of what is essential and universal. The 'Universal' Declaration of Human Rights and its twin covenants are supplemented, after all, by a treaty on the human rights of women. The 1993 Vienna World Conference on Human Rights felt the need to issue a conclusive statement that 'women's rights are human rights'. Seemingly neutral laws and principles may disadvantage women in their application. Human rights have addressed concerns of the public (masculine) sphere and have only lately begun to address rights violations prevalent in the private sphere, to which women are often relegated.

Respect for cultural difference can be a euphemism for denying women's equality and freedom, typically in the realms of sexuality, marriage, inheritance and reproduction (see box p 22). Women are often designated the role of guardians of culture, a defense against alien forms of 'progress' in a globalizing world. The 1995 Beijing Conference on Women rejected in unprecedented terms 'cultural' justifications for violating women's human rights.

Universalism vs cultural relativism

Is it true to say human rights are universal or is humanity too diverse? Are all values relative, dependent on culture? Universal human rights represent a search for the heart of human values. There may be certain minimum norms of human behavior – concerning say, genocide, torture, slavery, etc. – on which to build a workable consensus.

Another, often neglected, aspect of universality is the impartial and consistent application of rights standards as an indivisible whole. In US academic Micheline Ishay's view, 'cultural relativism is a recurrent product of a historical failure to promote universal rights discourses in practice, rather than a legitimate alternative to the comprehensive vision offered by a universal stand on justice.'[7] Double standards generate resentment. Reciprocity is required: rights that apply to you must apply to us too.

Harvard professor-turned-politician Michael Ignatieff argues that rights are universal because they define the universal interests of the powerless, demanding that power be exercised over them in ways

Las Madres de Plaza de Mayo

Argentina's Mothers of the Disappeared is one of a number of similar groups that have emerged since the 1970s in Latin American countries ruled by military dictatorships. 'Disappearances', a human rights violation without end, produced a new kind of human rights movement without end, as mothers mobilized on behalf of their loved ones who had been 'disappeared' by the regime. They began to hold demonstrations in the Plaza de Mayo, Buenos Aires, the central political space of the city and nation. Still today, women take themselves, their grief and mementos into a public space. The private sphere bursts into the public, demonstrating their indivisibility (see chapter 2). ∎

Female Genital Mutilation

Female genital mutilation (FGM) refers to a number of different procedures that alter the genitals – often of pre-pubescent girls unable to consent fully – for cultural reasons. FGM varies from a symbolic nick to radical removal of tissue and, in about 15 per cent of cases, sewing the vagina closed. Not mandated by any religion, it occurs mostly in Africa, but also in certain Asian, Middle Eastern and South American cultures and among their diaspora. It is often performed by women, commonly without anesthetic or sanitary precautions. It may be part of coming-of-age rituals for girls and intended to make them more acceptable for marriage.

Somalia-born model and author Waris Dirie, who has campaigned to end the disfiguring practice she suffered in her homeland, says: 'Mutilation is not a tradition – it's a crime that must be abolished.' She describes the ordeal she endured at age 5: 'I didn't move. I just shivered. There was no painkiller, no anesthesia, no nothing.'

The standard human rights position is that FGM is a violation of girls' and women's rights. As well as being painful and reducing sexual sensation, it can increase the risk of HIV transmission and cause other health problems related to urination, menstruation, sexual intercourse and childbirth. Infection or hemorrhaging can be fatal. The World Health Organization (WHO) estimates that over 135 million women worldwide have undergone FGM, with over two million more girls at risk every year.

Protecting girls and women from such complex cultural traditions isn't straightforward. While some countries have outlawed the practice, it may not be helpful to fine, jail or even (in Guinea) execute parents or practitioners. A heavy-handed approach can drive the practice underground, increasing risks to recipients, or lead to the circumcision of much younger girls, before they can object or run away. At the

that respect their autonomy as agents. Human rights arouse opposition because they challenge power-holders of various kinds. The main challenge to human rights' universality, therefore, is from the powerful.[11]

Arguments for cultural relativism suggest that rights are not universal, not compatible with all cultures and ought not to be imposed on all cultures, particularly where they may threaten cultural survival. In its most familiar guise, cultural relativism regards human rights as Western in origin and, at their worst, a form of cultural, political and even economic imperialism.

request of local partners, Amnesty's Stop Violence Against Women campaign doesn't press for legal bans.

FGM is one example of how non-legal methods of human rights promotion can be effective and culturally sensitive. Education and health programs are usually preferable, especially when designed and delivered by members of the affected culture (though this can lead to less severe forms of FGM rather than its elimination). Communities can develop alternate rites of passage to achieve the same cultural purposes without causing harm, as is occurring in Tanzania at the suggestion of Women Wake Up, a non-governmental organization (NGO). Simultaneous abolition throughout a village or 'marriage network' is ideal, so no-one is disadvantaged by being different. An INGO (international NGO) taking this approach in Senegal and Burkina Faso is *Tostan* ('Breakthrough'), which also recruits religious leaders to endorse its anti-FGM drives. Other grassroots NGOs find alternative employment for former FGM practitioners. ■

Amnesty International, 'What is female genital mutilation?' www.amnesty.org; WHO, 'Female genital mutilation factsheet' www.who.int; K Stevenson, 'Women changing their world' in *Human Rights Defender* (Amnesty International Australia, April/May 2005); T Tidwell Cullen, 'A woman's approach to ending a perilous rite of passage,' *Christian Science Monitor*, 8 June 2005. www.csmonitor.com; Integrated Regional Information Networks News, 'Sierra Leone: Female circumcision is a vote winner' (UN Office for the Co-ordination of Humanitarian Affairs 17 March 2005) www.irinnews.org; J Ensor, 'Linking Rights and Culture: Implications for Rights-Based Approaches' in P Gready & J Ensor (eds), *Reinventing Development? Translating Rights-Based Approaches from Theory into Practice* (Zed Books 2005). *The Associated Press*.

Such claims need to be questioned, just as claims to universality need to be justified. Who is speaking on behalf of the culture? Who benefits from such claims? At whose cost? And are they genuinely interested in protecting cultural diversity?

For human rights to work, we need to be able to identify as human and recognize the humanity of

'The universal nature of [all human] rights and freedoms is beyond question.' ■

2005 World Summit (paragraph 120).

others. It can't work if we are instead exclusively cultural beings without ethical obligations beyond our kin or cultural group. Some argue that it is natural and necessary to have limited boundaries of identification and obligation. Or that functioning ethical communities are intrinsically local. Others insist that solidarity with (if not beyond) the rest of our species – natural or not – is essential to human survival.[12] In this respect, universalism can be driven by fear as much as idealism. If the nation is itself an 'imagined community,'[13] can we not expand our imaginative horizons? Human rights provide the rationale and means by which to extend our moral horizons from kin to strangers.

And yet we are right to be concerned with cultural survival as well. To reject universal human rights as subordinate or inimical to culture is to assume either (a) that rights trample culture and/or (b) that human rights aren't up to the task of defending human diversity. Seen through a human rights prism, culture and community should be consensual and based on choice, both in defining their content and the ability to join or leave. Local activists campaign for human rights without rejecting their culture. They do not want Western culture, but certain freedoms within their own culture. Human rights do defend culture and cultural difference. Violations can be tackled without necessarily dismantling culture. Indeed, cultural rights are human rights (see box p 27).

Can cultural relativism and universalism be reconciled?
The UDHR was drafted by people of divergent cultural and philosophical backgrounds, including a US Roman Catholic, a Chinese Confucian philosopher, a French Zionist and a spokesperson for the Arab League (see chapter 2). The very fact we have in this book traced a multicultural history of human rights betrays a universalist assumption. At some level, human rights

'Asian values'

A particular form of cultural relativism that reached its apogée in the 1990s, 'Asian values' were said to include loyalty to family and nation, forgoing personal freedom for the sake of social stability and prosperity, the pursuit of academic and technological excellence, hard work and thrift – and that such values were incompatible with human rights. Proponents of Asian values, such as former PM of Singapore Lee Kuan Yew and former Malaysian PM Mahathir bin Mohamad, claimed authoritarian government is more culturally appropriate than democracy.

We might question the motives of such privileged powermongers. Counters Mahathir's beleaguered former deputy, Anwar Ibrahim: 'To say that freedom is Western or unAsian is to offend our traditions as well as our forefathers, who gave their lives in the struggle against tyranny and injustices.' Singapore's persecuted opposition leader Chee Soon Juan says it's racist to assert that Asians don't want human rights. As we shall see in chapter 4, there is a broad-based grassroots movement for human rights in Asia.

Indian economist Amartya Sen disputes the notion of uniform 'Asian values' as an over-generalization of the diverse cultures of the region. He finds no evidence of a necessary connection between authoritarian government and economic performance, and takes pains to distinguish universal human rights from Western hegemony. On the contrary; Western leaders, he argues, do too little to promote human rights in other countries. ■

A Ibrahim, 'Media and Society in Asia,' keynote speech to the Asian Press Forum (Hong Kong: 2 Dec. 1994); SJ Chee, 'Human rights: Dirty words in Singapore,' Activating Human Rights and Diversity conference (Byron Bay, Australia, 3 July 2003); A Sen, 'Human rights and Asian values: What Lee Kuan Yew and Le Peng don't understand about Asia', *New Republic 217(2-3)* (New York, 14 July 1997); A Sen, 'Democracy as a Universal Value,' *Journal of Democracy 10(3)* (1999) pp 3-17; C Brown, 'Universal Human Rights,' *International Journal of Human Rights 1(2)* (1997) pp 41-65.

have to be universal, or else they cannot be founded in our common humanity. There are a number of (related) ways of resolving tensions between universalism and cultural relativism, through which the twin streams of 'consensus' and 'evolution' flow.

1 *Universal content expressed in varied language*
There are different ways of expressing human rights in different cultures and any number of 'rights-like

concepts'. Charles Taylor (the Canadian philosopher, not the Liberian war criminal) argues that human rights are typically couched in Western-style language that may seem alien to other cultures, even if their content is universal. The word 'rights' itself may not translate readily into all languages, but alternatives can be found. Conversely, a common language of rights can help communicate and validate local struggles for a wider audience.[14]

2 Diversity founded on a common core
Human rights can be understood as minimum, common standards 'from which differing ideas of human flourishing can take root.'[11] They may be thought of as a 'floor' beneath which we will not sink. (Or should we aspire to more – human rights as a 'ceiling' or horizon of hope?) US scholar Jack Donnelly advocates a flexible approach to implementation. The abstract, universal substance of rights may be interpreted and implemented differently within reasonable boundaries.[15] For example, does the right to work mean the state must provide jobs or unemployment benefits, or something else again? Culture can be a defensible mechanism for selecting interpretations and forms of implementation.

3 Legal flexibility and pluralism
Aspects of international treaty law and, to a lesser extent, international customary law, tacitly endorse relativism. For example, states can refuse to recognize a particular right in a treaty by entering a reservation, declaration or derogation. The fact that global, regional and national legal frameworks protecting human rights co-exist demonstrates a legal accommodation of varied understandings of rights. In many countries, informal customary law operates in parallel with state law, although not always in the interests of human rights (see chapter 4).

4 Human rights are new to all cultures
The UN position is that 'universal human rights are a

What are cultural rights?

Human rights relating to cultural diversity and integrity include: the right to cultural participation; the right to enjoy the arts; conservation, development and diffusion of culture; protection of cultural heritage; freedom for creative activity; protection of persons belonging to ethnic, religious or linguistic minorities; freedom of assembly and association; the right to education; freedom of thought, conscience and religion; freedom of opinion and expression; and, as ever, the principle of non-discrimination. ■

D Ayton-Shenker, 'The challenge of human rights and cultural diversity', UN Background Note (UN Dept of Public Information 1995)

www.un.org/rights

modern achievement, new to all cultures. Human rights are neither representative of, nor oriented towards, one culture to the exclusion of others.'[16] Forms of oppression can be found in all cultures and religions. Human rights offer 'greater freedom, greater security from violence, from arbitrary treatment, from discrimination and oppression than humans have enjoyed at least in most major civilizations in history.'[5]

A rebuttal of the 'rights-are-Western' claim is similar: Western history is hardly the place to look for great models of rights practice, from the Crusades, witch trials, slavery and colonization through to the *Shoah* (Holocaust). Ignatieff argues that modern human rights, forged in the aftermath of this last event, are 'not so much the declaration of the superiority of European civilization, as a warning by Europeans that the rest of the world should not seek to reproduce its mistakes.'[11] In the 21st century, many Western nations are back-pedaling fast on matters of rights.

5 *Cross-cultural critique and consensus*

The search for equivalent, 'rights-like' concepts across cultures may be too static, overlooking the need or potential for change that is the aim of human rights. The risk is that human rights will simply reflect the lowest common denominator, masking the extent to which human rights and cultural norms and practices shape one another. Legal academics Susan Marks and Andrew Clapham prefer intra-cultural dialog and cross-cultural critique and exchange to a search for a narrow consensus, retaining human rights' potential as a driver of change. Cultures are seen not only comparatively, in terms of commonalities and difference, but also in terms of their internal contradictions and contested characters, and their capacity for change. Enlightened cultural interpretations by internal voices lend human rights cultural legitimacy, while cross-cultural exchange helps initiate and support such internal dynamics. The desired outcome is a universalism that harnesses dissent as a means of expanding and deepening the human rights consensus.[17]

6 *Socially constructed universalism*

Universalism can also be socially constructed and negotiated. Transnational advocacy networks, for example, are seen by US political scientists Margaret Keck and Kathryn Sikkink[18] not as conduits for Western values, but as political spaces for negotiation. Illustrative is the story of how, largely through a series of major UN conferences – particularly three during the UN Decade for Women (1975-85), plus the UN World Conferences on Human Rights in Vienna (1993) and on Women in Beijing (1995) – violence against women unified the women's movement, overcoming significant divisions and moving beyond a focus on discrimination. It did so by encompassing common experiences and structural problems but also difference, in terms of specific manifestations (from domestic violence to FGM). This campaign achieved significant normative advances in the 1990s. Networks, or the emerging foundations of global civil society, then, are sites where the human rights debate between universalism and cultural relativism is evolving and enabling.

Where to from here?

If the first human rights revolution occurred in the Enlightenment period, we are still feeling the effects of the second human rights revolution, in this globalization era. The pillars of this second revolution include engagement with different actors (beyond the state) in reformulated relationships (from critique to partnership, and often attempting to combine the two) and through new political struggles (see chapter 2).

Globalization means the causes of and solutions to human rights problems are complex and dispersed. One country sells weapons or buys diamonds that perpetuate conflict elsewhere; trade policies create poverty; aid conditionality allows external actors to dictate social policy and spending; borders closed to forced or voluntary migration shift the burden to other countries; environmental abuses cause distant disasters. At the same time, global action for human rights is now a reality.

Ignatieff argues that human rights enjoyed a heyday in the 1990s and that 11 September 2001 heralded the 'end of rights.' Governments the world over, most particularly the US, have turned their back on their human rights obligations in favor of national security[19] (and other objectives opportunistically pursued under the banner of the 'war on terror'). It's not at all clear, however, that a decline in states' commitment to human rights should be interpreted as a failure of the project as a whole. Cyclical patterns of decline and resurgence are evident in the history of human rights. But it is true that the nexus between the war on terrorism and terrorism itself (in all its guises) presents one of the greatest challenges to the human rights community today. Writes Ignatieff, 'The movement will have to engage in the battle of ideas: it has to challenge directly the claim that national security trumps human rights.' And more than asserting that

A powerful idea

respect for human rights is an essential component of an anti-terror strategy – both as an effective means and a cherished end – we must demonstrate that relationship. Despite the difficulties rights encounter at the macro political level, the second human rights revolution – our revolution – continues to make rights more and more relevant to different people.

1 O Ball, *Every Morning, Just like Coffee: Torture in Cameroon* (Medical Foundation for the Care of Victims of Torture 2002) pp 17-19. **2** M Freeman, *Human Rights: An Interdisciplinary Approach* (Polity 2002) p 12. **3** Art. 1, *Universal Declaration of Human Rights* (1948). **4** Amnesty International USA, *Amnesty Interactive: History and Atlas of Human Rights* CD-ROM (Voyager 1995). **5** C Taylor, 'Conditions of an unforced consensus on human rights,' in JR Bauer & DA Bell (eds), *The East Asian Challenge for Human Rights* (Cambridge University Press 1999) pp 124-44, 136. **6** SJ Hood, 'Rights hunting in non-Western traditions,' in LS Bell, AJ Nathan & I Peleg (eds), *Negotiating Culture and Human Rights* (Columbia University Press 2002) pp 110-11. **7** MR Ishay, *The History of Human Rights: From Ancient Times to the Globalization Era* (University of California Press 2004) pp 40, 11. **8** K Dalacoura, *Islam, Liberalism and Human Rights: Implications for International Relations* (IB Taurus 1998) p 47. **9** D Tutu, *No Future Without Forgiveness* (Pinter 1999). **10** M Wollstonecraft, *A Vindication of the Rights of Woman*, ed M Brody (Penguin Books 1992). **11** M Ignatieff, *Human Rights as Politics and Idolatry* (Princeton University Press 2001) pp 68 & 76, 95, 65. **12** M Walzer, *Spheres of Justice: A Defense of Pluralism and Equality* (Basic Books 1983). **13** B Anderson, *Imagined Communities: Reflections on the Origin and Spread of Nationalism* (Verso 1991). **14** J Cowan, M-B Dembour & R Wilson, 'Introduction' in J Cowan, M-B Dembour & R Wilson (eds), *Culture and Rights: An Anthropological Perspective* (Cambridge University Press 2001) pp 21-2. **15** J Donnelly, *International Human Rights* (Westview Press 1998) p 34. **16** D Ayton-Shenker, 'The Challenge of Human Rights and Cultural Diversity', United Nations Background Note, UN Department of Public Information (1995) www.un.org/rights **17** SR Marks & A Clapham, *International Human Rights Lexicon* (Cambridge University Press 2005) pp 388-98. Sudanese-US law professor Abdullahi Ahmed An-Na'im has been central to the emergence of this approach. See for example, 'Toward a Cross-Cultural Approach to Defining International Standards of Human Rights: The Meaning of Cruel, Inhuman or Degrading Treatment or Punishment' in AA An-Na'im (ed), *Human Rights in Cross-Cultural Perspective: A Quest for Consensus* (University of Pennsylvania Press 1992). **18** ME Keck & K Sikkink, *Activists Beyond Borders: Advocacy Networks in International Politics* (Cornell University Press: Ithaca 1998) pp 211-12, also 165-98. **19** M Ignatieff, 'Is the human rights era ending?' *The New York Times* 5 February 2002. www.mtholyoke.edu

2 Different rights make a whole

'The ideal of free human beings enjoying civil and political freedom and freedom from fear and want can only be achieved if conditions are created whereby everyone may enjoy his civil and political rights, as well as his economic, social and cultural rights.'

INTERNATIONAL COVENANT ON CIVIL AND POLITICAL RIGHTS (ICCPR) AND THE INTERNATIONAL COVENANT ON ECONOMIC, SOCIAL AND CULTURAL RIGHTS (ICESCR) 1966.

'All human rights are universal, indivisible and interdependent and interrelated. The international community must treat human rights globally in a fair and equal manner, on the same footing, and with the same emphasis.'

VIENNA DECLARATION AND PROGRAM OF ACTION, WORLD CONFERENCE ON HUMAN RIGHTS, 1993, REAFFIRMED BY THE UN'S 2005 WORLD SUMMIT IN NEW YORK (PARA. 121).

Human rights touch almost every aspect of life. Taken as a whole, they suggest a way of living together in peace, dignity and freedom. Attempts are made to categorize rights, however, and give some priority over others. At the same time, innovative connections are breathing new vigor into them.

DESPITE CONSISTENT REAFFIRMATION by the international community that all human rights are intertwined (indivisible), few states have accepted in practice their indivisibility. It is often economic, social and cultural rights that get left behind. Western thinking has tended to prize political and civil rights – such as freedom of expression and association, freedom from torture, slavery, arbitrary arrest and detention – above economic, social and cultural rights, such as the rights to work, education, health and housing. Proponents of so-called 'Asian values' (see chapter 1) and of the 'full-belly thesis' do the reverse, arguing that civil and political rights are secondary to economic, social and cultural rights. These very common divisions of rights are not only erroneous, but destructive to the pursuit of that ideal of universal human dignity that human rights represent. Some non-governmental organizations (NGOs) that have traditionally overlooked economic, social and cultural rights have come to embrace the doctrine of indivisibility, notably the biggest of them all, Amnesty International, with an overhaul of its mandate in 2001.[1]

The unity of human rights derives from the unity of the human person. Twentieth-century New York psychologist Abraham Maslow proposed a hierarchy of needs, in which our bodily need for food and shelter is more fundamental than intellectual, aesthetic or

A human rights reading of famine

Economist Amartya Sen's theory of famine as a failure of entitlement describes a complex interplay of rights as necessary to any meaningful analysis of food insecurity. Household food security is affected by education, employment, transport, housing, health and food prices. There is a crucial role for civil and political rights too. Sen claims that there's never been a famine in a functioning, multi-party democracy. A free press and freedom of expression, transparent and accountable government and so forth, are the best early-warning system and spur governments to action when famine looms. The mass starvation that resulted from Mao's 'Great Leap Forward' in China in 1958-61, by contrast, occurred in a context of political repression.

A Sen, *Development as Freedom* (Oxford University Press 2001); J Drèze, A Sen & A Hussain (eds), *The Political Economy of Hunger: Selected Essays* (Clarendon Press 1995).

A contract to prevent famine

'The idea of a social or political contract dedicated to famine prevention constitutes an attempt to infuse social and economic rights into spiritual pursuits. This cannot explain people who will go without food or income, or will give up their life, for the sake of religious belief or political goals. The political right to vote or to freedom of opinion are more fully enjoyed by the person who also enjoys their economic right to education. Conversely, Nobel Prize-winning economist Amartya Sen attests that these same political rights can help ensure the right to food and freedom from hunger. Writer and activist Alex de Waal goes further to advocate a more comprehensive political contract (see box).

History of the UDHR

An appreciation of history is essential for understanding where we are today. The UN was not the first international body to attempt to codify and protect human rights. The forerunner of the UN, the League of Nations, had a go in 1919. The International Labour Organization (ILO), also founded in 1919,

civil liberties, ie to explain why some social and economic rights are considered sufficiently important that they are guaranteed by political process. A "political contract"... is the result of a popular movement successfully articulating a new right, and forcing a reluctant government to comply with its claims... Following the success of each of these "primary movements", governments have recognized that maintaining their legitimacy rests on respecting certain democratic rights. These gains are defended by the "secondary activism" of specialists such as journalists, lawyers, elected representatives, etc, who have (at least in principle) the opportunity to fall back upon secondary mobilization. Famine is so self-evidently wrong and so visible that it readily offers itself as a political cause. It has often provided the impulse for mass mobilization. Sometimes it has been a scandal among the political classes. Occasionally, it has been both, but only rarely has it proved the basis for an enduring coalition that can enforce a long-term change in governments' political priorities... In such cases one can truly speak of an anti-famine political contract.' ■

A de Waal, *Famine Crimes: Politics and the Disaster Relief Industry in Africa* (James Currey 1997) pp 11-12.

still defends workers' rights. Earlier still, the Hague and Geneva conventions were drafted to protect rights during armed conflict (see chapter 3).

The UDHR is the seminal document of the modern (post-World War Two) era of human rights. It was a 'distillation of nearly two hundred years of efforts to articulate the most basic human goods and values in terms of rights.'[2] Hailed by the UN as 'the most exhaustive documentation on the subject of human rights ever assembled,'[3] it remains the highest moral and legal authority in human rights.

Authored by a group of experts from across the globe, in consultation with such luminaries as Mahatma Gandhi, the UDHR draws on many sources from a variety of cultural, religious and legal traditions.[4] Canadian law professor John Humphrey wrote more than three-quarters of the original draft of the *Declaration*, after months of exhaustive study of existing world literature on the subject. Perhaps his most significant contribution was to include economic and social rights in his draft (contrary to the common assumption that these rights were unfamiliar to the West, and a Soviet insertion). No member state opposed these rights in principle. The then Labour Government of the UK acquiesced and Harry Truman's Democrat government of the US gave its full support. These rights had a strong basis in US legal and political culture, evident in Roosevelt's New Deal, for instance (see box), as well as the *National Labor Relations Act* and the *Social Security Act*. The US position was to change dramatically, however, when Republican Dwight Eisenhower became President in 1952: the Cold War had begun.

By the time the UDHR was presented to the UN General Assembly for adoption in 1948, the political atmosphere was, in the words of John Humphrey, 'charged to the point of explosion by the Cold War with irrelevant recriminations coming from both

The Four Freedoms

'In the future days which we seek to make secure, we look forward to a world founded upon four essential human freedoms. The first is freedom of speech and expression – everywhere in the world. The second is freedom of every person to worship God in his own way – everywhere in the world. The third is freedom from want, which, translated into world terms, means economic understandings which will secure to every nation a healthy peacetime life for its inhabitants – everywhere in the world.

The fourth is freedom from fear, which, translated into world terms, means a world-wide reduction of armaments to such a point and in such a thorough fashion that no nation will be in a position to commit an act of physical aggression against any neighbor – anywhere in the world.

That is no vision of a distant millennium. It is a definite basis for a kind of world attainable in our own time and generation. That kind of world is the very antithesis of the so-called "new order" of tyranny which the dictators seek to create with the crash of a bomb.' ∎

President Franklin D Roosevelt in a speech to the US Congress on 6 January 1941.

sides.'[5] None the less, on 10 December 1948, the UDHR was adopted unanimously, with abstentions from the Soviet bloc, apartheid South Africa and Saudi Arabia.

The Cold War and the twin covenants

The visionaries behind the *Universal Declaration of Human Rights* always intended that it should be 'completed' by a binding covenant. Declarations carry moral weight only – and the weight of the UDHR is hard to overestimate – but in international law only covenants or conventions are binding upon ratifying countries (although today, the UDHR has customary law status, see chapter 4).

Pressed by the Soviet bloc and some developing states, such as Chile, the General Assembly confirmed in 1950 by means of the so-called 'Unity Resolution' that the proposed covenant *would* include economic rights. The following year, Western nations, along with some other developing countries, such as India, 'went on the offensive'[6] to secure separate covenants with, critically, separate implementation or enforcement mechanisms for the two supposedly different sets of rights. They succeeded in getting a new resolution passed dictating this outcome.

Canadian academic Craig Scott has studied UN debates leading up to this 'Separation Resolution'. He identifies three broad reasons for the separation:

1 *Implementation-based reasons:*

The allegedly different nature of civil and political rights and economic, social and cultural rights were taken to mean that the latter are non-justiciable, and therefore need different procedures of implementation. We shall return to this question of justiciability shortly.

2 *Ideological or political reasons:*

The Cold War period 'saw international politics and ideology join hands as never before ... While delegations did not expressly invoke' politics or ideology for or against a single covenant, they often accused their opponents of such base motives. Over all, the debate fell along an East–West axis, with developing countries that were UN members at the time going either way, often according to Cold War loyalties.

Classical Western liberal philosophy has tended to separate politics and economics.[7] Perhaps the Cartesian dichotomy of body and soul is also evident, especially in the implied prizing of civil and political ideals above the demands of the body. For the Soviets, the emphasis on the material was, of course, Marxist in origin.

3 *Pragmatic reasons:*

A number of practical arguments were advanced in favor of two covenants, for example:

- the work of the ILO and other specialized agencies of the UN might be duplicated if economic rights were included;

- the codification of economic rights was deemed to require a lot more work, while a draft covenant on civil and political rights was ready to go. Putting all rights in one covenant would cause an intolerable delay. (As it happened, both covenants took a long time to finalize, and were adopted simultaneously in 1966, 18 years after the UDHR);

- it was feared a combined covenant would not attract enough support for it to enter into force, rendering the whole exercise pointless. The US and others threatened that they would not sign or ratify a treaty containing economic rights. Two separate covenants would maximize support and progress, as virtually all states would be willing to sign at least one. Ironically, the US did not ratify the ICCPR until 1992.

All of these reasons, whatever their merits in 1951, carry far less weight today. Yet many misconceptions about economic, social and cultural rights persist.

A case for indivisibility

The most commonly asserted essential or 'natural' differences between the two sets of rights (assertions that give way under closer scrutiny) are summerized in the box overleaf.

These dichotomies are interrelated criticisms, usually of economic, social and cultural rights. It's not that these distinctions are never true, but the traditional separation of economic, social and cultural rights from civil and political rights is misleading and unhelpful. Let's have a look at some arguments in favor of this kind of indivisibility, then explore some newer interpretations of the concept.

First, to the accusation that economic, social and cultural rights are inherently different (and inferior or less legitimate) because they are **imprecise**; that is, it is supposedly unclear what states' obligations are in relation to economic, social and cultural rights, and when these rights have been violated. But think

---

A false dichotomy of rights

Economic, social and cultural rights	Civil and political rights
positive	negative
resource-intensive	cost-free
progressive	immediate
vague	precise
unmanageably complex	manageable
ideologically divisive/political	non-ideological/non-political
socialist	capitalist
non-justiciable	justiciable
aspirations or goals	'real' or 'legal' rights

C Scott, 'The Interdependence and Permeability of Human Rights Norms: Towards a Partial Fusion of the International Covenants on Human Rights,' Osgoode Hall Law Journal, Vol 27 (1989).

---

of civil and political rights, say the right to privacy: what are the state's precise obligations here? Advances in biomedicine challenge our assumptions about the right to life – when it begins and when it ends. What is the precise nature of our right to vote?

The point is not that the exact nature of a nation's electoral system should be dictated by the UN, rather that imprecision is not unique to economic, social and cultural rights. The task of identifying the minimum core content and, if you like, the additional, 'supplemental' content, of our human rights remains an ongoing challenge. Rights that may have seemed straightforward in 1951 yield new complexity, while the 'fuzzy' economic, social and cultural rights are getting clearer and more precise, especially since the end of the Cold War. The experts monitoring the ICESCR – the Committee on Economic, Social and Cultural Rights – have expanded their reach and resources by collaborating with UN agencies such as the WHO and UNESCO to thrash out the detail of these rights. (See the Committee's General Comments on the right to housing, food, education,

health, water, work, etc. at: www.ohchr.org/english/
bodies/cescr/comments.htm). Meanwhile, important
progress has been made in the jurisprudence of places
such as India and South Africa on the right to food
and housing (see box p 104).

And so to the issue of **justiciability**. A right is said
to be justiciable if its violation can be determined
in a court or similar legal proceedings. The failure
of a government to provide judicial or other remedy
for a particular violation does not mean the related
right is non-justiciable. Housing rights specialist
Scott Leckie contends that 'all human rights contain
components that are justiciable in any courtroom of
the world.'[8] He blames persistent, gross violations
on 'problems of perception and resolve, rather than
any inevitable limitation of law or jurisprudence.'
For instance, 'when someone is tortured or when a
person's right to speak freely is restricted, observers
almost unconsciously hold the state responsible.
However, when people die of hunger or thirst, or
when thousands of urban poor and rural dwellers

Delivering the right to health

'There is nothing in international human rights law that says a State's
health care system must be public in the sense that it must be a
nationalized health service, such as the UK's National Health Service.
The right to health places an obligation on the State to ensure that
there is a health care system delivering right-to-health outcomes
to all. Whatever system a State chooses, its operation must be
consistent with other human rights and democratic principles. So
a good right to health outcome (for example, low or negligible HIV
prevalence) that is achieved in a way inconsistent with other human
rights (for example, through the incarceration of all those with HIV/
AIDS) is unacceptable.

The right to health approach is evidence-based: What delivers the
right to health for all, including those living in poverty? . . . A right to
health approach brings rigorous analysis – you might say discipline
– to national and international health policy-making.' ■

Paul Hunt, UN Special Rapporteur on the Right to Health (*Essex
Human Rights Review* Vol 2, No 1, 2004).

are evicted from their homes, the world still tends to blame nameless economic or 'developmental' forces, or the simple inevitability of human deprivation.'[8] Or it blames the victim.[9] As we shall see in chapter 5, legal battles are not essential to every human rights struggle, but it is not the case that one set of rights has an inferior legal standing.

Following from the contention that civil and political rights engender so-called **negative** obligations on the state – that is, the obligation to refrain from, say, torture – while economic, social and cultural rights impose a **positive** obligation – to provide, say, social security – are the related charges that economic, social and cultural rights are **expensive** for a government to honor, while the hands-off approach of civil and political rights is **inexpensive**. This notion persists, it seems, because protection of our civil and political rights by the state is so taken for granted (in many countries) so as to render it almost invisible. The classic bourgeois right to property (which appears in the UDHR, but was sufficiently controversial to be dropped from both covenants) is typically protected by a state police force, which also protects, and indeed may violate, our right to life and security of person. Other expensive civil rights obligations on the state include effective and just legal and judicial systems, and free, fair elections. On the other hand, there are economic, social and cultural rights that call for non-intervention by the state, such as the right to form trade unions. Similarly, the right to non-discriminatory access to education or health care costs nothing.

All human rights 'entail ,a complex, multi-layered obligations structure.'[6] All rights have positive and negative dimensions. A formula requiring the state to respect, protect and fulfill our rights encapsulates these dimensions (see box).

And here we encounter the purported distinction

between the two sets of rights which is explicit in the covenants themselves: the notion that civil and political rights can be implemented **immediately**, while fulfillment of economic, social and cultural rights will take time. While the implementation mechanisms of the two covenants differ – there currently being an individual complaints mechanism for civil and political rights only – both covenants require participating countries to submit periodic reports to the UN on their progress in implementation, thus revealing a **progressive** aspect to both sets of rights. Certainly today, with the increasingly sophisticated explication of rights, it is clear they all impose immediate obligations, both negative and positive – that is, minimum or core standards or thresholds – while the supplementary obligations attached to all rights, may require progressive realization, as resources and other conditions allow.

Finally, are economic rights communist and political rights capitalist? 'The West may have neglected economic and social rights in the nineteenth and early twentieth centuries. But that anyone looking at the welfare states of Western Europe over the past half century can be expected to take such a description of the Western approach seriously, to put it bluntly, boggles the mind... Conversely, as we saw in 1989, citizens in the former Soviet bloc, when given

---

Respect, protect and fulfill

Governments have three kinds of obligations in relation to human rights:

Respect – refrain from actively violating human rights (an immediate, 'negative' obligation);

Protect – act to prevent violations by third parties (say, by regulating the activities of transnational corporations or TNCs); and

Fulfill (or promote) – act to attain the most rapid enjoyment of rights for all (by appropriate legislative, administrative, budgetary, judicial and other positive means). ■

the opportunity, demanded their civil and political rights.'[10] Since political theorist Jack Donnelly wrote these words, the 'war on terror' has demonstrated that civil and political rights are not as cherished (by some) in the capitalist West as was once thought.

The doctrine of rights indivisibility is often a hollow mantra. For many, it is a daily reality. Only by exercising such rights as freedom of association and expression did the people of Cochabamba, Bolivia, assert their right to water,[11] as people do in myriad ways every day, all over the world.

'New' holistic indivisibility

With the second human rights revolution comes fresh perspectives on indivisibility; new ways of bringing together what might once have been considered irreconcilable opposites in human rights discourse and practice. Relationships between actors are redrawn and ways of working re-examined, in an

---

Priorities not hierarchies

Australian-US human rights expert Philip Alston warns against taking indivisibility too far:

'If every possible human rights element is deemed to be essential or necessary then nothing will be treated as though it is truly important. A list of requirements that is too demanding or ignores trade-offs and dilemmas is unlikely to be taken seriously by practitioners who are operating under major resource and time constraints and are faced with competing priorities and the need to make difficult choices. Two caveats are in order at this point. First, the call for prioritizing is not to suggest that any obvious violation of rights can be ignored... Second, contextually identified priorities must be distinguished from fixed hierarchies.'

Priorities, where necessary, should adhere to core concepts (such as reasonable attempts at progressive realization) and principles (such as non-discrimination, equality and participation). ∎

P Alston, 'Ships Passing in the Night: The Current State of the Human Rights and Development Debate Seen Through the Lens of the Millennium Development Goals', *Human Rights Quarterly 27(3)* (2005) p 807.

---

effort to find the most effective modes of action in a globalized world.

Means/ends

It is often, if not always, the case that the means by which human rights goals are pursued are just as important as the desired ends. The *way* an NGO works, or a system of democracy is established, or a trial is conducted will have an impact on the desirability, durability and the legitimacy (and, perhaps, morality) of the outcome. Process and outcome must be congruent. There are a number of human rights values or principles that can guide our design of processes intended to secure human rights outcomes. Not a fixed list, these principles include: equality, justice, non-discrimination, participation, accountability, transparency, diversity and peace.

Public/private

As we saw in chapter 1, feminists have decried the emphasis on rights that are evident in the public realm to the neglect of rights abused in private. Where the domestic, in particular, is construed as a woman's place and as private – that is, no business of the state (or law or rights) – women and children suffer. Much of women's work and most violence against women occur in the private sphere. Many issues of

---

Rights *experienced* as indivisible

'In explaining poverty, poor men and women often express a sense of hopelessness, powerlessness, humiliation and marginalization... In Cameroon poverty is characterized as "a feeling of powerlessness and an inability to make themselves heard".... Lack of voice and power is experienced not only in interactions with the state, but also in poor people's interactions with the market, landlords, bankers, moneylenders and employers.' ■

D Narayan with R Patel, K Schafft, A Rademacher & S Koch-Schulte, *Voices of the Poor: Can Anyone Hear Us?* (World Bank/ Oxford University Press: New York 2000) pp 39-40.

concern to women, such as reproductive rights, are not traditionally seen as matters of human rights. Feminists have asked: if torture committed by the state is a human rights violation, what is the same act perpetrated by a husband upon a wife? As the slogan goes, the personal is political. That is, the public and private spheres are interdependent and indivisible (see box p 102).

Violence against women, which is perpetrated mostly by partners and ex-partners in 'private' contexts, has been a unifying theme in the fight for women's human rights. The growth of a global campaign against this pandemic of violence (see box) is evident in the building of support for the campaign at successive UN conferences, from Nairobi in 1985 to Beijing ten years later. In 1992 the UN committee governing the *Convention on the Elimination of All Forms of Discrimination Against Women* (CEDAW) interpreted the treaty as imposing on states a positive obligation to take action in relation to violence against women. In 1993 the UN adopted a *Declaration on the Elimination of Violence Against Women* and in 1994 created the post of Special Rapporteur on Violence Against Women. The Organization of American States (OAS) also has a binding covenant on the subject. No state can now claim that gender violence is beyond its responsibility.

State and non-state actors

Many of us think of rights violations as something that governments do. This central tradition in human rights reflects social contract theory (discussed in Chapter 1). However, natural law theory also understands abuses as breaches of the 'natural order of things,' regardless of who commits them. Some of the earliest international human rights law – such as the many treaties of the ILO protecting workers' rights since 1919, and the *Slavery Convention* of 1926 prohibiting the activities of non-state actors in the slave trade

– reflects this understanding of human rights as something anyone can violate. The expectation of the UDHR is that 'every individual and every organ of society' will work towards the universal realization of rights.

Thus, human rights ought to be protected – and can be violated – by states, by multilateral organizations composed of states (which may or may not individually be party to human rights treaties), and by non-state entities (which do not sign treaties).[12] Former UN High Commissioner for Human Rights Sergio Vieira de Mello described the World Bank, International Monetary Fund (IMF) and the World Trade Organization (WTO) as 'some of the fundamental obstacles to the realization of rights.'[13] Yet existing UN mechanisms for the protection of human rights (see chapter 4) focus on state violations, and as such are inadequate to the task of monitoring and evaluating the human rights performance of multilateral and non-state entities.

In 2003 the UN tried to correct this omission by issuing *Norms on the Responsibilities of Transnational Corporations and other Businesses on Human Rights* and a commentary thereon. These Norms assert states' primary responsibility to respect,

---

Violence against women

At least one out of every three women around the world has been beaten, coerced into sex, or otherwise abused in her lifetime. The abuser is usually someone known to her. In 2002 the Council of Europe declared violence against women a public health emergency and a major cause of death and disability for women aged 16 to 44 years. A World Bank report estimated that violence was as serious a cause of death and incapacity among women of reproductive age as cancer, and a greater cause of ill-health than traffic accidents and malaria combined. ■

UN Dept of Public Information, 'Behind Closed Doors: Violence Against Women' in *Ten Stories the World Should Hear More About* (New York 2005) www.un.org

protect and fulfil human rights, noting that part of this responsibility involves keeping private enterprise in line. It describes how TNCs and other businesses can foster economic well-being, development and technological advancement, or they can violate human rights 'through their core business practices and operations, including employment practices, environmental policies, relationships with suppliers and consumers, interactions with Governments and other activities.' Another UN initiative in this area is its Global Compact, which challenges business leaders to abide by ten principles covering human rights, labor rights, the environment and corruption. Voluntary adherence to this and other corporate codes of conduct needs to be bolstered by legal and non-legal measures, such as consumer pressure.

Many see in the era of globalization the decline of the nation state. The reality is more complex, however, with decentralization and privatization redistributing resources and power between state and non-state actors and within the state (for example, to local government). Human rights need to respond to this challenge.

Action at home/abroad

A related aspect of indivisibility is the obligation on states and others to act outside their jurisdiction, that is, a moral and legal imperative to promote human rights in other countries, too. Many states are simply incapable of fulfilling human rights without international assistance. Others actively violate rights in heinous ways. The International Council on Human Rights Policy in Geneva has published a good deal on the subject of extra-national duties.[14] In Chapter 3 we shall examine the difficult question of how far states should go in the pursuit of rights compliance abroad.

The whole issue raises thorny questions of state sovereignty: that is, the idea that all states are equal and independent and should be treated as such. Experience amply demonstrates that, in reality, this is far from the case. Some states have greater power and dominate others. In this globalized world, states' sovereignty is also infringed by the power of corporations and multilateral bodies. Bullying by powerful states – whether to accept unfavorable trade conditions or to clean up a shameful human rights record – is often a cause of great resentment. International criticism may be justified, of course, but so may a weak state's efforts to determine its own affairs. Self-determination (of peoples) is a human right, but that's not the same thing as state sovereignty. A modern understanding of sovereignty might emphasize responsibility rather than authority.

NGOs and activists too need to work to increase awareness and lobby the government at home, as well as working on other countries – to avoid the impression that human rights problems are always elsewhere, and because the two strategies are fundamentally linked and complementary.

Local/global
Many NGOs now work at various levels, recognizing the importance of local interventions to people's immediate lives, but also that wider contexts and structures require action at the national and international level. Digging wells will be of limited benefit if structural adjustment policies force governments to cut health and education budgets; urgent interventions to halt torture and extrajudicial executions need to take place alongside efforts to stem the arms trade.

Top-down/bottom-up
It's easy to get the impression that human rights are handed down and adjudicated from on-high, whether by the UN or, say, a national constitution. But few human rights win recognition and respect without

pressure from below. The American and French revolutions of the eighteenth century, the socialist mobilization of workers in the nineteenth century and the feminist and anti-imperialist gains of the 20th century were all bottom-up social movements that demanded and won human rights protection at the highest levels. Alongside this bottom-up mobilization around rights, top-down processes can lead to contests over rights adjudication and meaning.

Working with/against

Can activists who picket Nike stores for exploiting vulnerable workers also meet with Nike board members for constructive discussion? Could they even work for TNCs with integrity? How can a resource-extraction company be expected to respect indigenous rights if they don't have knowledgeable and competent people on staff who can conduct community consultations or draft rights-sensitive social policy? A prominent Australian conservationist copped flack from both greenies and loggers in 2004 when she accepted a top job with the forest industry, which continues to fell old-growth forest in Victoria. Was it a coup for the industry or for the environment? To make the World

---

State sovereignty

'Around the world, people are far more apt to be harmed by their own than by other governments. Harm results from numerous forms of misgovernment – political and military repression, graft, judicial corruption, economic discrimination against minorities and so on. Such behavior clearly offends against the norm of sovereignty. The norm nevertheless protects abusive governments and corrupt élites, who can appeal to sovereignty and insist on non-interference in their internal affairs whenever they face international pressure to reform. For this reason, some have called sovereignty a "refuge for scoundrels".' ■

International Council on Human Rights Policy, *Duties sans Frontières: Human Rights and Global Social Justice* (2003) p 48.

Linking local and global: an Oxfam example

'Creating more space for the representatives of Southern NGOs in international fora, in order to link local activists and global decision makers more effectively, is one of the strategies pursued in the Oxfam International Campaign to *Make Trade Fair*. Often a long-term process of building capacity and trust precedes such linking. The case of Sahelian cotton farmers, who, together with Oxfam International, succeeded in voicing their views effectively at the WTO meeting in Cancún in 2003, is a good illustration of this process... The unequal power relations that constrain human development can be confronted more forcefully when international principles and instruments of human rights can be brought to bear on national legislation, and in turn citizens can draw on both levels to demand their rights... Working on these issues from the local level upwards, building the awareness and capacity to promote human rights, and joining forces and linking different actors and different levels are strategies that – when done well – give expression to Oxfam's quest for global equity.' ■

M Brouwer, H Grady, V Traore & D Wordofa, 'The Experiences of Oxfam International and its Affiliates in Rights-Based Programming and Campaigning' in P Gready & J Ensor (eds), *Reinventing Development? Translating Rights-Based Approaches from Theory into Practice* (Zed Books 2005) pp 67 & 76.

Bank live by its professed poverty agenda, should we organize to protest or prepare to collaborate? The answer is probably 'both-and'. These questions are complex, as illustrated in the box on p 51.

In truth, such partnerships and alliances are not new. NGOs and civil society have for some time formed part of state delegations to international meetings and worked closely with sympathetic states drafting legal norms. While the Red Cross, for example, attempts persuasion, others choose the traditional human rights approach: denunciation. Both 'modes of action' may be necessary and complementary. A third approach is substitution.[15] Rather than acting as a check on the state, some NGOs, notably in the development and humanitarian sectors, provide services (sometimes as formal sub-contractors) that could be considered the responsibility of states. Human rights NGOs may, for example, provide training for police. Such relationships carry dangers for civil society: they

Owning rights, retaining meaning

'[Human rights] has infiltrated the United Nations and other international/regional institutions, governments, civil society organisations and NGOs. It is banging on the door of presidents, the private sphere, non-state actors and international financial institutions. The practice of development, humanitarianism, public health, foreign policy and more is being influenced in many, and different, ways by its rhetoric and methods. But with this development has come a new challenge, the challenge of "mainstreaming", of ownership of human rights, of what an ideology used by so many to secure such different ends actually means any more, of converting a shared vocabulary into shared values.' ■

P Gready, 'The Politics of Human Rights' in *Third World Quarterly*
24(4) 2003, pp 749-50.

may risk co-option or complicity in abuse, facilitate economic globalization, undermine the developing state and become financially dependent.

These relationships indicate an important change in human rights activist agendas, one which law professor Richard Falk describes as a shift from 'anti-statism' to 'collaborative activism'.[16] This strategy has enabled NGOs and civil society, in alliance with core groups of sympathetic states (and despite US opposition), to establish innovative governance mechanisms, such as the Ottawa Treaty banning anti-personnel landmines, and the International Criminal Court.

Individual rights/group rights

Human rights are sometimes said to be too individualistic. Certainly, many rights are for the individual, but many imply relationships or are group rights, which only find meaning collectively. Cultural rights, in particular, make little sense as individual rights, since culture is necessarily a shared experience. What do I gain from the right to speak Kurdish, for example, if I know no other Kurdish speakers?

Human rights are an asset to any democratic system. Upholding as they do the interests of any minority (individuals or groups) as equal to those of the majority, they serve a check-and-balance function; a foil to the potential tyranny of majoritarian democracy and utilitarianism (the greatest good for the greatest number). Many minority groups – such as indigenous peoples, sexual minorities and religious, ethnic or linguistic minorities – have embraced human rights as a way of defending themselves against abuse and discrimination. In 2005 the UN created the post of Independent Expert on Minority Issues to engage in dialog with both governments and minorities worldwide to advance minority rights.

Working with non-state actors

'The pharmaceutical sector has some duties in relation to the right to health . . . But we have a long way to go to clarify the scope of these duties and then to figure out what they mean in the real world of patents, drug pricing, health research and development, Joint Public Private Initiatives in the field of health, and so on. I [have] made the following suggestions: First, a small group of so-called experts from the human rights community and from the pharmaceutical sector should meet three or four times a year for two years to talk through these issues in a serious manner, supported by solid research, and without grandstanding. At the end of two years, the experts should produce a report that identifies common ground as well as differences of opinion. In a way, this will be a confidence-building exercise – presently, it seems to me, there is much misunderstanding between the human rights and pharmaceutical communities. This exercise should be followed by a three-year experimental period during which an *ad hoc* group of independent experts examines, through the prism of the right to health, the activities of some pharmaceutical companies. The *ad hoc* group should publish short, accessible, constructive and balanced reports on what they find. In other words, here we have an embryonic form of human rights accountability being extended to some parts of the pharmaceutical sector... It is tempting to give facile, glib responses to these complex issues. I think it is very important to resist this temptation. These are challenging, far-reaching and important issues that demand intellectual rigor, interdisciplinary collaboration, and imagination.' ■

Paul Hunt, UN Special Rapporteur on the Right to Health, *Essex Human Rights Review 2(1)* (2004).

Different rights make a whole

New frontiers
Where different conceptions of rights indivisibility demonstrate the depth of human rights, the new frontiers into which the discipline is moving show their range and breadth. Their power and potential is being proven in new arenas in the fight for justice, equality and freedom. Here are just a few examples.

Rights-based approaches to development
Human rights have given the development project, now decades old, a much-needed shot in the arm. Leading humanitarian and development agencies – such as UNICEF, CARE and Oxfam – as well as governments and other donors have recognized the links between poverty and rights denial.[17] A rights framework emphasizes power relations and the role of the state, processes as well as outcomes, and accountability. And more than economic rights, a vital part of rights-based development is the defense of civil and political rights, giving impoverished people a voice and a role in the development agencies that propose to work with them as well as in governmental and international fora.

Medical rights
To be a moral actor in the twenty-first century involves managing various moral codes, of which human rights is one. Professional groups and organizations mobilize, appropriate and reinterpret rights primarily because they are useful. Medical ethics, for example, have traditionally emphasized duties, which tacitly assume doctors' benevolence and authority. A 'revolution in medical ethics' has opened the way to medical rights, which hold that 'the locus of medical authority ought to lie with patients rather than physicians.'[18]

Human rights and the environment
Given that human life and welfare ultimately depend on the rest of the ecosystem, human rights and the

When human rights and environment collide

The endangered population of orangutans on the Indonesian island of Sumatra was not directly affected by the tsunami of December 2004, but with an estimated 8.5 million cubic meters (over 300 million cubic feet) of timber needed to rebuild Banda Aceh, their dwindling forest habitat is under unprecedented pressure. People have a right to housing and the other infrastructure that support health, work and education. Must orangutans bear the cost? Environmentalists pressed for international aid to include a massive influx of imported plantation timber. The orangutan's chances of survival remain perilous. ■

Borneo Orangutan Survival Foundation, 'What has been the impact of the Tsunami on orangutans?' (Melbourne 2005) www.orangutans.com.au

environment are indivisible. As with other rights, there may be times when the interests of humans and of the environment conflict and we may want to question whether human rights 'trump' the rights of other species (see box above). Very often, though, our interests will coincide, as all species benefit from a clean environment and sustainable resource management. Conversely, it is often the case that human rights violations in their turn damage the environment.[19] It should be possible to 'go beyond reductionist concepts of "mankind first" or "ecology first".'[20] After all, an ecosystem is, by definition, interdependent.

Environmental rights fall into two categories: (1) efforts to prevent and clean up environmental pollutants, from heavy metals to nuclear waste – we could think of this as a right to a clean or healthy environment – and (2) democratic and non-discriminatory use of and access to natural resources by present and future generations – that is, an equal right to environmental 'goods'.

A parallel approach is taken by the environmental justice movement, which opposes resource appropriation (typical of the consume-and-waste

> ## Indivisibility of environment, health and equity
> 'Rights to access, use and manage natural resources are inextricably linked to the rights of health and economic welfare... Both aspects of the environmental rights agenda are fundamentally concerned with health, whether the threats stem from a polluted environment or from loss of access to the natural resources that families need to sustain themselves. Both are also concerned with equity, as it is those groups already marginalized politically and economically whose rights are most consistently transgressed.' ∎
> BD Ratner, 'Environmental Rights as a Matter of Survival,' *Human Rights Dialogue* (Spring 2004).

societies of the industrialized North) and displaced injustice (the shifting of environmental hazards, spatially and temporally, to the poor and powerless and to future generations). Environmental justice connects the social and environmental aspects of sustainable development. Environmental hazard/ resource inequalities are linked to other inequalities, such as unequal access to information and decision making processes, income, employment opportunities, health and education, creating cumulative injustices across issues, space and time. Any potential solution requires the framing of justice and human rights as procedural and substantive, international and intergenerational.[21]

In essence, the new indivisibility is a call for competent governance, from the local to the global level, so that one hand does not take away what the other hand gives. How can aid, debt (relief) and trade work together rather than at odds with one another? Do we really want major international players, such as TNCs, to have rights but no responsibilities? Does a woman enjoy her basic human rights if the most dangerous place for her is her own home? The new indivisibility is about breaking down artificial barriers, no longer relevant in the era of globalization, and seeking to make all rights relevant to all people in all places where they live and work. The new frontiers outlined here are also about keeping rights relevant; they indicate the vibrant, dynamic nature of human rights today.

1 http://web.amnesty.org 2 M Glendon, 'John P. Humphrey and the Drafting of the UDHR' in *Journal of the History of International Law*, Vol 2, 2000 3 'International Bill of Rights to be Drafted,' *UN Weekly Bulletin* (17 June 1947) p 639. 4 MA Glendon, *A World Made New: Eleanor Roosevelt and the Universal Declaration of Human Rights* (Random House 2001). 5 JP Humphrey, *Human Rights and the United Nations: A Great Adventure* (Transnational Publishers 1984). 6 C Scott, 'The Interdependence and Permeability of Human Rights Norms: Towards a Partial Fusion of the International Covenants on Human Rights,' *Osgoode Hall Law Journal*, Vol 27, 1989, p 835. 7 F Jhabvala, 'On Human Rights and the Socio-Economic Context,' *Netherlands International Law Review*, No 149, 1984. 8 S Leckie 'Another Step Towards Indivisibility: Identifying the Key Features of Violations of Economic, Social and Cultural Rights,' *Human Rights Quarterly* 20(1) 1998, pp 105, 82. 9 S Cohen, *States of Denial: Knowing About Atrocities and Suffering* (Polity 2001). 10 J Donnelly, *International Human Rights* (Westview Press 1998). 11 M López Levy, 'The damn water is ours!' *New Internationalist* No 338, September 2001. www.newint.org 12 International Council on Human Rights Policy, *Beyond Voluntarism: Human Rights and the Developing International Legal Obligations of Companies* (2002). 13 S Vieira de Mello, 'Five questions for the human rights field', in *Sur International Journal on Human Rights* No 1, 2004, pp 165-71, www.surjournal.org/eng 14 www.ichrp.org 15 International Committee of the Red Cross, *Strengthening Protection in War: A Search for Professional Standards: Summary of Discussions Among Human Rights and Humanitarian Organizations* (Imprint 2001). 16 R Falk, 'Human Rights and Global Civil Society: On the Law of Unintended Effects' in P Gready (ed.), *Fighting for Human Rights* (Routledge 2004) pp 33-53. 17 P Gready & J Ensor (eds), *Reinventing Development? Translating Rights-Based Approaches from Theory into Practice* (Zed Books 2005). 18 C Wellman, *The Proliferation of Rights: Moral Progress or Empty Rhetoric?* (Westview Press 1999) p 133. 19 Preamble, Draft Principles on Human Rights and the Environment (1994). 20 F Zohra Ksentini, 'Review of Further Developments in Fields with which the Sub-Commission has been Concerned Human Rights and the Environment', UN Commission on Human Rights (1994). 21 C Stephens & S Bullock, 'Civil Society and Environmental Justice' in P Gready (ed), *Fighting for Human Rights* (Routledge 2004) pp 134-52.

3 Rights in war and armed conflict

What happens to human rights when fighting breaks out? International humanitarian law protects human rights during that least humanitarian of human activities: war. Major crimes committed during armed conflict can now be punished through international criminal law. But law is not the only way of ending impunity, building peace and protecting human rights. Other approaches can be compatible and effective.

THERE ARE AT this moment about 40 armed conflicts being fought in nearly 30 countries, many of which never make the news. Some countries have multiple conflicts, notably India, Indonesia, Burma and Nigeria. A number of current conflicts have each resulted in more than 100,000 deaths, such as Algeria, Colombia, the Democratic Republic of Congo (DRC), Kashmir, Rwanda, Somalia and Sudan. Other countries, such as

Countries affected by armed conflict

Algeria	DRC	Sudan	India (&	Sri Lanka	Russia/
Burundi	Liberia	Uganda	Kashmir)	Solomon	Chechnya
Central	Nigeria	Afghanistan	Nepal	Islands	Iran
African	Rwanda	Burma	North Korea	Turkey	Iraq
Republic	Senegal	China	Pakistan	Kosovo	Israel/
Côte d'Ivoire	Somalia	Indonesia	Philippines	Colombia	Palestine

G Tieman & O Ball, *Blood on the Planet: The Who, What, Where and When of Armed Conflict in the World Today* (Uniting Church in Australia. 2004).

A grim inheritance

'Tracing the lives of children in Chechnya was like descending through the levels of hell. Close to the bottom were children broken by physical as well as psychological wounds. Amina, her thin fingers wrapped around the hospital-bed railing in pain, sobbed almost absentmindedly, as if she had forgotten how to draw an ordinary breath. From her small pelvis a thicket of tubes sprouted, replacing the functions of organs torn apart by shrapnel.

In the primitive village hospital ward 12-year-old Said [lay] with his face to the wall, rigid with shock and rage, his newly-amputated arm bound up just below the shoulder.

By the time they are 15, the doctor told me in a whisper, [boys like Said] will be dedicated fighters. If Chechnya does not win its independence from Russia, they will continue the struggle to the death. Beyond, to the next generation.' ■

O Ward, 'Letter from Chechnya: The Lost Generation,' *New Internationalist* 281, July 1996 p 3.

Iraq, Afghanistan and Angola, have suffered hundreds of thousands of deaths in recent years.

Of the hundreds of thousands of people who die each year as a result of armed conflict, most are civilians. The Red Cross estimates that 10 per cent of those killed in World War One were civilians. By World War Two, that figure had risen to nearly 50 per cent. Since the end of the Cold War, 90 per cent of those killed in conflict have been non-combatants. The main casualties are the unarmed, women, children and the elderly. Children account for at least half of all civilian casualties. Many people die not at the hands of weapons, but from disease and famine resulting from the disruption to health services, essential infrastructure and agriculture.

Escalating civilian casualties are due in part to new technologies and reduced public tolerance for military deaths, leading to strategies that tend to increase civilian tolls. Arms-length aerial warfare, for instance, has largely supplanted brief, bloody battles between opposing armies and navies. There has also been a rise in guerrilla warfare in which fighters merge with, and

---

My neighbor

Woman, 38, from Teslić, Bosnia-Herzogovina: 'We were very afraid that if some of their people got killed, they would no longer say hello to us, as if we were the ones who did it. Then our neighbors started to disturb us... My cousin was killed in his home... A neighbor killed him in the middle of the night, because his brother was killed on the front line. Even though my cousin was a Muslim volunteering in the Serbian army, wounded when fighting for his village...

[Reflecting on her own rape, the woman continues] when I... recognized him as a neighbor I felt even worse, I got more afraid. So often he had sat at our place, drank coffee with us. He had even worked for me. He raped me... That is why I left, I couldn't defend myself. He could do anything he wanted.' ∎

J Mertus, J Tesanovic, H Metikos & R Boric (eds), *The Suitcase: Refugee Voices from Bosnia and Croatia* (University of California Press 1997) pp 28-30.

---

thereby endanger, civilian populations. Civil populations are also mobilized, sometimes forcibly, to turn on one another (see box).

Beyond the death, injury, grief and psychological trauma associated with the violence of war, the impact of conflict includes large-scale forced displacement, the abuse of children as soldiers and sex slaves, disruption of development and of the supply of essential goods and services, property damage, destruction of the environment and the violation of many human rights.

Human rights amid the fighting

Depending on where you live, you may know the Red Cross or Red Crescent for its thrift stores, blood banks and First Aid courses, or as a neutral party in conflict zones, providing medical aid and reuniting families. It also has an important role as keeper of international humanitarian law (IHL). Governments are allowed by law to derogate (beg off) from certain human rights commitments – such as the right to privacy – but only as 'strictly required' by public emergencies that 'threaten the life of the nation', such as war. By contrast, some human rights can never lawfully be suspended, including the right to life, to freedom of thought and the prohibitions on torture and slavery. It is exactly at such times of armed conflict, when some rights may be curtailed, that IHL comes into play to add an extra layer of human rights protection.

In 1859 Henri Dunant, a Swiss merchant on a business trip in northern Italy, was horrified to witness an appalling battle near Solferino. His efforts to aid some of the 40,000 wounded soldiers, and to take a dying message to one young man's parents in Lyon were to change his life and a lot more besides.[1] Determined to end unnecessary suffering in war, he established the International Committee of the Red Cross (ICRC), which, a mere 18 months later, had launched the first of the Geneva Conventions and with it, modern IHL.

Dunant was not the first to think of trying to 'humanize' armed conflict. The Chinese were debating treatment of prisoners of war (POWs) as early as 500 BCE. At around the same time the Manu Law of War, a Hindu legal manuscript, prohibited the use of poison and poisonous weapons, as did the ancient Greeks and Romans.[2] Illustrating again the 'consensus' and 'historical evolution' narratives converging, the Red Cross has counted over 500 recorded texts

International Committee of the Red Cross, *International Humanitarian Law: Answers to your Questions* (Geneva 2002) p 11; M Sassoli, A Bouvier, NA Dupic & LM Olson, *How Does Law Protect in War?* (ICRC 1999) p 145; Iraq Coalition Casualty Count http:// casualties.org/oif/; Iraq Body Count project www.iraqbodycount.net

Civilian deaths in war

WWI – 10% civilian

WWII – 48%

Korean War – 83%

American War in Vietnam – 95%

current Iraq war – 84%

attempting to regulate hostilities prior to modern IHL.[3] Perhaps the earliest debate on the unacceptability of 'collateral damage' is found in the Torah.[4] The Qur'an also advocates respect for one's adversaries.

International humanitarian law

The Geneva Conventions, dating from 1864, are the core of IHL. The four conventions protect soldiers, sailors, POWs and civilians, respectively. IHL attempts to regulate both the means and the methods of war. It cannot and does not seek to prevent armed conflict, but it does attempt to prohibit 'superfluous' or 'unnecessary' suffering[5] and to limit what suffering does occur to the direct protagonists in the conflict, that is, armed combatants.

It is not simple, theoretically or practically, to regulate war. There are obvious contradictions in asserting the right to life, even during war, while permitting certain kinds of killings, namely those inflicted by armed combatants upon each other. But a pragmatic humanitarian can see the benefits of having warring parties agree to limit their behavior. Warring parties, too, should see that respecting IHL is one way of protecting their own citizens. How the US treats detainees in Guantánamo Bay or Abu Ghraib, for instance, may have a bearing on how its own nationals (and allies) are treated when the tables are turned. In any case, the Geneva Conventions apply to

---

Enemies by accident

'War is in no way a relationship of man with man but a relationship between States, in which individuals are enemies only by accident; not as men, nor even as citizens, but as soldiers... Since the object of war is to destroy the enemy State, it is legitimate to kill the latter's defenders as long as they are carrying arms; but as soon as they lay them down and surrender, they cease to be enemies or agents of the enemy, and again become mere men, and it is no longer legitimate to take their lives.' ■

Jean-Jacques Rousseau, *The Social Contract* (1762).

all parties (state and non-state) in all cases of armed conflict 'in all circumstances,'[6] whether or not the other side respects those laws.

Key provisions of the Geneva Conventions and Additional Protocols are:

1 Civilians, as well as sick or wounded combatants, are entitled to respect for their life and their moral and physical integrity.

2 Wounded, sick or surrendered enemies must not be injured or killed but cared for.

3 The dignity and rights of any captured combatants or civilians must be respected. They are entitled to correspond with their family and receive relief.

4 Fundamental judicial guarantees remain intact during war. No-one shall be held responsible for an act they have not committed. Torture, corporal punishment and cruel or degrading treatment are prohibited.

5 Weapons or methods of warfare that cause unnecessary losses or excessive suffering are illegal.

6 Only military targets may be attacked. Civilians, their property and essential infrastructure (such as dams, crops and power stations) must not be attacked.[7]

From Nuremberg to Sierra Leone

Grave breaches of IHL are war crimes. There have been major developments in international criminal law since World War Two, propelled by major atrocities. At the end of that war, the Allies tried 22 Germans, including politicians, military leaders and industrialists, at a military tribunal established for the purpose at Nuremberg (Nürnberg).

It was not the only post-World War Two trial. The other major one was of 29 Japanese in Tokyo in 1946; there were also hundreds of 'subsidiary' trials. Often derided as 'victors' justice', it is not true that the Allies did not try their own as well. The US, for example, tried hundreds of its own personnel, over one hundred of whom were sentenced to death and executed.

That captured enemies were tried at all was a significant advance in human rights. Stalin and Churchill preferred simply to take them out and shoot them, as had been British policy regarding captured enemy leaders in the last two years of the war.[8] Roosevelt and Truman argued successfully for a trial. The US judge appointed to head Nuremberg, Robert Jackson, marveled 'that four great nations, flushed with victory and stung with injury, stay the hand of vengeance and voluntarily submit their captive enemies to the judgement of the law'. And, determined as the Allies were to try only those certain to be convicted, three of the defendants were acquitted.

Nuremberg and the other trials of this period are not beyond criticism. Carefully avoiding charges that mirrored Allied crimes too closely (such as aerial

---

What are crimes against humanity?

The 'widespread or systematic' perpetration of any of the following acts against a civilian population:
- Murder
- Extermination
- Enslavement
- Deportation or forcible transfer of population
- Imprisonment or other severe deprivation of physical liberty in violation of international law
- Torture
- Rape, sexual slavery, enforced prostitution, forced pregnancy, enforced sterilization or any other form of sexual violence of comparable gravity
- Persecution against any identifiable group or collectivity on political, racial, national, ethnic, cultural, religious, gender or other grounds... in connection with any crime within the jurisdiction of the International Criminal Court
- Enforced disappearance of persons
- The crime of apartheid
- Other inhumane acts of a similar character intentionally causing great suffering, or serious injury to body or to mental or physical health. ∎

Rome Statute of the International Criminal Court (1998).

---

bombing), the Allies invented some new crimes with which to charge the defendants, breaching a fundamental legal principle that says you shouldn't be tried for something that wasn't illegal at the time you did it. Creating a new category of 'crimes against humanity', Jackson argued that 'civilization cannot tolerate their being ignored, because it cannot survive their being repeated.' The legal status of the crimes newly codified by the Nuremberg Charter of 1945 – crimes against peace, crimes against humanity and genocide – has not been questioned since.

The Nuremberg Tribunal was a watershed in the fight against impunity for flagrant human rights violations for a number of reasons:

* It held individuals responsible for the actions of states and other collective entities.
* It underlined concrete duties we all have under international (as well as national) law.
* It overruled 'just following orders' as a defense.
* By prosecuting private industrialists for manufacturing arms and using forced labor from the concentration camps, it demonstrated the culpability of non-state actors in the violation of human rights, whether independently or by supporting state action.
* It set a significant precedent for intervention by the 'international community' in the internal affairs of a sovereign nation where serious human rights abuses are at stake, in this case the extermination of Germans by Germans.

After Tokyo and the other trials dealing with World War Two, international criminal law suffered a hiatus for some 50 years (during which time international human rights law made a leap forward; see chapter 4). There were no further international tribunals until the UN Security Council created the International Criminal Tribunal for the former Yugoslavia (ICTY) in 1993 and the International Criminal Tribunal for Rwanda (ICTR) in 1994. No one would have predicted in 1993 that Slobodan Milošević, the first serving head of state indicted for international crimes, would be in custody in The Hague in 2001. Nor would anyone have predicted that nearly 20 indicted suspects would hand themselves over to the ICTY, as occurred in 2005. None of this could have happened had the Tribunal not existed in the first place.

Sierra Leone's Special Court is a somewhat different beast; a combination of both national and international judges applying national and international law. Cambodia and East Timor, for their part, created 'internationalized domestic tribunals' with UN input.

The International Criminal Court

A permanent international court for the trial of international war crimes has been a long time coming. The 1948 Genocide Convention, the 1949 (revised) Geneva Conventions, the 1973 Apartheid Convention and the 1984 Convention Against Torture each reinforced the idea of individual criminal responsibility first established at Nuremberg. The International Criminal Court (ICC) established in The Hague under the 1998 Rome Statute can hear charges of genocide, war crimes and crimes against humanity. A fourth crime prosecuted at Nuremberg, that of aggression or against peace, appears on the Rome Statute, but remains a latent provision so long as its definition cannot be agreed. The advent of 'pre-emptive war' in the case of Iraq highlights the difficulties surrounding this issue.

The ICC's pre-trial chambers have examined crimes alleged to have occurred in Uganda, DRC and the Central African Republic – at the request of the governments of those countries. Contrary to scaremongering in some quarters, the ICC is strictly a back-up to national courts. The 'principle of complementarity' means that no-one will be hauled off to The Hague if their own government is willing and able to try them. For example, British soldiers charged with abusing Iraqi detainees will be tried in Britain under the UK's *International Criminal Court Act 2001*. Either the accused's country of nationality or the country in which the crime was committed must have ratified the ICC statute. Only the UN Security Council has the power to act independently of this requirement, and has done so, referring the situation in Darfur to the ICC for investigation, even though Sudan is not a member of the Court. It is interesting to note that despite the Bush Administration's hostility to the Court, the US chose not to veto this case.

The ICC differs from Nuremberg in a number of key ways. It will consciously seek to deliver fair trials to both 'winners' and 'losers'. The maximum penalty is life imprisonment – capital punishment being a human rights violation. It will not have retrospective powers; only crimes committed since 1 July 2002 can be tried at the ICC (or since whatever date after this the relevant state acceded to the court's statute). The ICC must have female and male judges, a measure that has important ramifications for the prosecution of crimes against women.

Rape

Rape is a human rights violation under the rubric of torture and cruel, inhuman or degrading treatment. In wartime, reprisals of any kind against civilian populations are explicitly prohibited in Geneva law, as are 'rape, enforced prostitution and any form of indecent assault', slavery and 'collective punishments', whether committed by combatants or civilians.[9]

Tens of thousands of mainly Muslim women and girls were systematically raped during the wars in the former Yugoslavia. In 2001 the ICTY found mass rape and sexual enslavement to be a crime against humanity, convicting three Bosnian Serb paramilitary officers of the rape and enslavement of Bosnian Muslim

---

First-ever genocide conviction

Fifty years after the Genocide Convention opened for signature, Rwandan town mayor Jean-Paul Akayesu became the first person to be convicted of genocide in an international court. In this instance, his crime was not mass killing but involvement in the mass rape of women belonging to a particular ethnic group (Tutsis) during the 1994 genocide in Rwanda. His prosecution was also notable as a departure from 'mechanical' definitions of the crime of rape towards the 'how' and 'why', more in line with the experiences of victims. Akayesu was not charged with committing acts of sexual violence himself, but with inciting and encouraging others to rape. The ICTR sentenced him to life imprisonment. ■

www.ictr.org; N Pillay, 'Sexual Violence in Times of Conflict: The Jurisprudence of the International Criminal Tribunal for Rwanda,' in S Chesterman (ed.), *Civilians in War* (Lynne Rienner, Colorado 2001).

---

women at Foca prison camp in 1992. The ICTR found the rape of women belonging to a particular ethnic group to constitute genocide (see box). Rape and forced pregnancy are defined as crimes against humanity in the founding statute of the ICC.[10]

As in other jurisdictions, there can be obstacles to

What rape means

Q: When you say 'rape', what exactly do you mean?

A: In the Yugoslav language in those days, which is now Bosnian, there is a word, *silo*, which means power, strength. To me, that very word, *silovanje*, because I was a child of 15. So they used force, power, strength to bring me there, and that means everything. Everything I went through, as well as the other girls, occurred not through my will or my acquiescence but by the use of force, power and strength...

Q: How did it make you feel while you were in Karaman's house?

A: Awful, dreadful, helpless. But at the same time I felt dignified and proud... We girls, children, were hopeless. They were men under arms and they used force. But simply I did not want to be subdued. They would often describe us as slaves, but I wouldn't accept that. ■

Testimony 2423-4 in the Foca trial

J Mertus, 'Shouting from the bottom of the well: The impact of international trials for wartime rape on women's agency' in P Gready (ed.), *Political Transition: Politics and Cultures* (Pluto Press 2003) pp 240-1.

---

trying crimes of sexual violence in international fora and even successful prosecutions may have an ambiguous impact on survivors.[11] A lack of political will and the perception that rape cases are too difficult to prove leads to rape charges being overlooked, as in the original Akayesu indictment. ICTR Judge Navanethem Pillay found that prosecutors weren't even asking witnesses about sexual violence. Such insensitivities combined with inadequate witness protection and cultural taboos may leave survivors afraid or unwilling to testify.

What is universal jurisdiction?

One of the more exciting things to happen in international law (if you go for that sort of thing) is the evolution of universal jurisdiction. It means that the most serious violations of human rights – war crimes, genocide and crimes against humanity – can now be tried at national level as well as internationally. This might be the national courts of the perpetrator, the national courts of the country where the crime was committed, the national courts of the victims or the national courts of the country where the perpetrator is arrested.[12] A national court's jurisdiction (reach) can be made 'universal' by its government passing laws declaring the court competent to try international crimes committed elsewhere. Extradition treaties then add to the court's effectiveness. Belgium's unprecedented legislation was a leading example (see box p 68), until US pressure led to it being repealed. The more countries that invoke universal jurisdiction – a practical expression of human solidarity[13] found in some form in over a hundred countries – the fewer opportunities for impunity and the greater the deterrent.

Candidates for this type of prosecution include Jean-Claude 'Baby Doc' Duvalier, ruler of Haiti 1971-86, now presumed to reside in France; Alfredo

---

Justice delayed

In September 1982 Lebanese troops (trained and equipped by Israel) entered adjacent refugee camps Sabra and Shatila in then-Israeli-occupied Beirut and slaughtered hundreds, possibly thousands, of the mostly Palestinian residents. Israeli troops surrounded the camps throughout the massacre, preventing escape. Ariel Sharon, then Israeli Defense Minister, was in command of the Lebanese militia. Israel itself named Sharon as personally responsible, and forced him to resign. The UN General Assembly called it an act of genocide.

Twenty-three survivors of the massacre now living in Belgium, which had universal jurisdiction legislation between 1993 and 2003, mounted a case against Sharon and others, even though neither the accused nor the victims are Belgian and the crimes did not occur there. The case against Sharon was dismissed when the Belgian Court of Cassation deemed him, by then Israeli head of state, immune from prosecution.

Others wanted in Brussels for international crimes include Cuban President Fidel Castro, deposed Iraqi President Saddam Hussein, Côte d'Ivoire President Laurent Gbagbo and, until his death, Palestinian leader Yasser Arafat.

In spite of the repeal of the legislation, investigations into the crimes of former Chadian dictator Hissène Habré continued and in September 2005 he was indicted. Senegal, which has him under house arrest in Dakar, is not expected to hand him over to the Belgian court for trial. ∎

UN GA Resolution 37/123 of 16 December 1982: 'The situation in the Middle East' www.un.org; T Sebastian, 'New "evidence" in Sharon trial,' BBC News Online, 8 May 2002, news.bbc.co.uk; BBC News, 'Belgium opens way for Sharon trial', 15 January 2000, news.bbc.co.uk; Human Rights Watch, 'Belgium: Questions and Answers on the "Anti-Atrocity" Law', June 2003, www.hrw.org; A Penketh, 'Africa's Pinochet' faces extradition and trial for crimes against humanity,' *The Independent*, 30 September 2005, news.independent.co.uk

Stroessner, Paraguayan dictator 1954-89, now in Brazil; and Mengistu Haile Mariam, dictator of Ethiopia 1977-91 and now in Zimbabwe. Thatcher and Kissinger are both said to restrict their international travel on legal advice concerning the risk of extradition for war crimes prosecution (see box). US Defense Secretary Donald Rumsfeld will be likewise limited in his movements when he leaves

Fugitives from justice

The case against Henry Kissinger

The still-fêted octogenarian was national security adviser to US President Nixon (1969-73) and Secretary of State to both Nixon and President Ford (1973-77). He is said to have been unnerved by the arrest of former Chilean President Pinochet in 1998. Anglo-US journalist Christopher Hitchens details Kissinger's crimes, including:

1 The mass killing of civilians in Indochina;
2 Collusion in mass murder and assassination in Bangladesh;
3 Planning the murder of a senior government figure in Chile;
4 Involvement in a plan to murder the President of Cyprus;
5 Inciting and enabling genocide in Timor Leste; and
6 Involvement in a plan to kidnap and murder a journalist in Washington, DC.

C Hitchens, *The Trial of Henry Kissinger* (Verso 2002).

The case against Charles Taylor

Warlord Charles Taylor won the Liberian presidential election in 1997 with a campaign song that went, 'He killed my Ma, he killed my Pa, I'll vote for him.' His rule of this war-torn West African nation was marked by violence. Not content with afflicting Liberia, he fuelled war in Côte d'Ivoire and Sierra Leone, in the last case by supporting the Revolutionary United Front (RUF), a rebel group whose atrocities shocked the world. Taylor, in turn, profited from the RUF's control of 'conflict diamonds'.

He is now wanted on 17 counts of war crimes and crimes against humanity, including killings, mutilations, rape, sexual slavery, abduction, using child soldiers and forced labor. The UN-backed Special Court for Sierra Leone issued a warrant for Taylor's arrest in 2003. When he was forced from office later that year, Nigeria offered him sanctuary until 2006 when, under pressure from the US and some 300 African and international civil society groups, Nigeria finally handed him over to be tried. ∎

Amnesty International press release, 'Sierra Leone: UN rights chief should call for Taylor's surrender' (London, 13 July 2005) web.amnesty. org; IRIN news, 'Taylor disappears from exile mansion' (Abuja, 28 March 2006) www.alertnet.org; Reuters, 'Liberia's Taylor arrested in northern Nigeria' (Maiduguri, Nigeria 29 March 2006) www.alertnet.org

office for having authorized torture.[14] Universal jurisdiction legislation could be used to prosecute anyone, however, not just political leaders. Certain drawbacks of universal jurisdiction are evident, such as access to witnesses and evidence and the potential for politically motivated prosecutions.

Rights in war and armed conflict

The Pinochet precedent

The indictment of former Chilean President Augusto Pinochet by Spanish judge Baltasar Garzón, and his arrest in London in October 1998, provide another example of universal jurisdiction at work. That Pinochet was not, in the end, extradited and may never actually stand trial for thousands of killings, disappearances and cases of torture during his time as Commander-in-Chief of the Chilean armed forces does not lessen the importance of the precedent set. This case bucked the tradition of legal immunity for heads of state and other high officials.

The UK House of Lords decided Pinochet could be extradited for trial on the grounds that to uphold his claim to immunity would be incompatible with the Convention Against Torture, which Chile, Spain and the UK had all ratified. To do otherwise, they argued, would be to accept torture as a proper function of the state. The Special Court for Sierra Leone has since drawn on this precedent to reject Charles Taylor's claim to immunity.

Efforts to try the octogenarian Pinochet for various crimes in Chilean courts since his return in 2000 have been stymied by claims of immunity and ill health. At the time of writing, he was facing prosecution in Chile for his involvement in Operation Colombo – the abduction and killing of more than 100 political prisoners in 1975.

Alternative and complementary measures

Criminal prosecution is not the only or perhaps even the best response to grave human rights abuses. For every individual who stands trial, many others do not. And arguments can be mounted against holding a trial in particular circumstances, such as where there may be scarce resources, a politicized or inadequate judiciary, or fragile peace and democracy. A number of alternatives occur in practice, some less

For the record

Paulina: 'When I heard his voice last night, the first thought that rushed through my head, what I've been thinking all these years... Doing to them, systematically, minute by minute, instrument by instrument, what they did to me... I was horrified at myself. That I should have so much hatred inside – but it was the only way to fall asleep at night... But I began to realize that wasn't what I really wanted – something that physical. And you know what conclusion I came to, the only thing I really want? [*Brief pause.*] I want him to confess. I want him to sit in front of that cassette recorder and tell me what he did – not just to me, everything, to everybody – and then have him write it out in his own handwriting and sign it and I would keep a copy forever – with all the information, the names and data, all the details. That's what I want.' ■

A Dorfman, *Death and the Maiden* (Nick Hern Books 1994) Act II.

desirable than others. They include: ignoring what has happened, exacting extra-judicial justice (eg killing, jailing or exiling those deemed responsible without a trial), issuing a blanket amnesty, brokering diplomatic or political deals that trade amnesty for peace or some other objective, establishing a 'truth and reconciliation' type process, or pursuing other informal or indigenous means of adjudication and enforcement and/or restoration. More than one of these may operate in tandem. Which is the best approach (or combination of approaches) in any specific instance will depend on the value placed on different objectives: punishment and justice, deterrence, peace and stability, exposing truth and correcting/creating an historical record, smoothing domestic or international relations, promoting reconciliation.

The 1994 genocide in Rwanda, perpetrated by huge numbers of people, presents an impossible situation for any court. More than ten years after the genocide, some 80,000 suspects remain detained under harsh conditions awaiting trial. *Gacaca* ('grassroots') courts were introduced as a modified form of community or local justice. They contain both a retributive and a

---

Truth as justice and liberation

Irene Mxinwa, mother of one of the 'Guguletu Seven' killed by police in Cape Town in March 1986, reflects on her experience testifying at a human rights violations hearing:

'The Truth Commission was so powerful... we felt that here is the place where we can actually find justice... It made us feel at home. It created a safe environment where we can actually feel that we are human beings and we have dignity, we have a name, we have a face... not only a story.

The way in which it brings the truth out, it is healing and you find justice in it... The way they conduct their hearings, their methods that they use to get information actually sets you free... the way that the truth came out, you could actually see and feel justice.' ■

---

restorative justice dimension, and operate alongside the ICTR and national courts. The scale of this experiment is huge, as over 500,000 people may ultimately be tried by *gacaca* courts. Amnesty International has questioned the procedural fairness of the *gacaca* system,[15] but the only alternative may be to release all those awaiting trial.

Democratic South Africa faced a problem of comparable magnitude. Part of its response to the complex and longstanding crime of apartheid was to establish a Truth and Reconciliation Commission, in which victims had a forum to be heard while perpetrators were offered amnesty in exchange for full disclosure. The South African Commission is the best known of its kind, but not the first (see table).

Can human rights and justice be reconciled with peace?

There's a caricature of human rights defenders as legalistic, moral(istic), adversarial enforcers of (absolute) norms. Peace practitioners, by contrast, favor dialog, seeking solutions through negotiation and compromise. What can they have in common? Peace and justice may be interdependent, but they can also be in tension. Pursuit of one may obstruct the other. Both may need to be compromised. There are no easy answers.

Some truth commissions around the world

1977	India
1982	Bolivia
1983	Argentina
1985	Zimbabwe
1986	Philippines, Uganda
1990	Chad, Chile
1991	Nepal
1992	El Salvador, Germany
1993	Rwanda
1994	Guatemala, Haiti, Malawi, Sri Lanka
1995	Burundi, South Africa
1996	Ecuador
1999	Nigeria
2000	Peru, Sierra Leone, South Korea, Uruguay
2001	Panama & Timor Leste
2002	Ghana
2004	Morocco
2005	Liberia

Conflict resolution specialists Ghalib Galant and Michelle Parlevliet see an important role for human rights in conflict resolution and describe the synergy thus:[16]

1 Human rights abuses are both symptoms and causes of violent conflict.

2 A sustained denial of human rights is a structural cause of high-intensity conflict because basic human needs are not met.

3 Institutionalised respect for human rights and the structural accommodation of diversity is a primary

'To a large degree, the rehabilitation of [Uruguayan and Brazilian society], to the extent that it has occurred, was accomplished by the torture victims themselves. These victims – hollowed-out, burnt-out shells – came alive once again by testifying to the truth of their own experiences. And the truth, to a degree, has set both themselves and their societies free.' ■

L Weschler, A Miracle, a Universe: Settling Accounts with
Torturers (Pantheon Books 1990) p 246.

form of conflict prevention.

4 The prescriptive approach of human rights actors must be combined with the facilitative approach of conflict management practitioners for the effective and sustainable resolution of intra-state conflict.

5 Conflict management can function as an alternative to litigation in dealing with rights-related conflicts.

6 Whereas human rights and justice *per se* are non-negotiable, the application and interpretation of rights and justice are negotiable within the context of a negotiated settlement.

Rights of refugees and internally displaced persons

The UN created a High Commissioner for Refugees (the UNHCR) in 1950 and the following year agreed a Convention Relating to the Status of Refugees (the 'Refugee Convention') to address post-war refugee movements in Europe. By 1967 it was clear that refugees were neither solely a product of World War Two, nor a problem confined to Europe, and a Protocol was added to broaden the original Convention to apply to all refugees.

According to the UN Convention, a refugee is any person who, 'owing to well-founded fear of being persecuted for reasons of race, religion, nationality, membership of a particular social group or political opinion, is outside the country of his nationality and is unable, or owing to such fear, is unwilling to avail himself of the protection of that country; or who, not having a nationality and being outside the country of his former habitual residence as a result of such events, is unable, or owing to such fear, is unwilling to return to it.' The 145 countries that have ratified this treaty are obliged to accept refugees and not return them (*refouler*) to any place where they might face the same or similar dangers. Moreover, refugees should enjoy at least the same rights in their new country as any other legally resident foreigner, including freedom of thought, religion and movement, health care and education and the right to work.

An obvious difficulty with the UN Convention definition, which none the less remains the most widely accepted today, is the requirement that a refugee demonstrate how they were targeted for persecution on grounds of their race, religion, nationality, social group or political opinion. Of course, many civilians are endangered by war and upheaval without anyone stopping to ask their political or religious beliefs. Of the five grounds, the category 'social group' is the least often applied due to its vagueness. Attempts have been made to include persecuted sexual minorities and victims of gender-based violence as members of a 'social group', with varying success. France, the Netherlands, the US and Canada, for instance, recognize female genital mutilation (FGM) as grounds for refugee status.

In 1969 Africa agreed its own refugee convention, which extended the definition of a refugee to include people fleeing 'external aggression, occupation, foreign domination or events seriously disturbing public order.'[17] A Central American statement on refugees, the 1984 Cartagena Declaration, refers to flight from armed conflict, generalized violence, massive violations of human rights or 'other circumstances which have disturbed the public order,' which could be construed as including environmental refugees fleeing, say, an earthquake or industrial accident. Slow-moving environmental catastrophes such as desertification and rising sealevels produce refugees that may not fit even this definition.

International law, having set the parameters, leaves it to states to decide who is and isn't a refugee. Methods of determination ought to be 'rapid, flexible and liberal... recognizing how difficult it often is to document persecution,' and ought to include a review mechanism.[18] A claimant needn't demonstrate that

---

Unwanted and dangerous

'S' of Doboj, Bosnia, aged 54: 'I try to read the German newspapers as infrequently as possible now, but every once in a while I buy one and take a look. There are so many stories about how Germany is flooded with refugees, especially those refugees from Bosnia. I read about why we are a danger, why we should be kept out. Meanwhile, I – the one with the college education – take care of their children and clean their houses. Never before in my life did I ever step foot anywhere where I was not wanted. I do not recognize what I have become.' ■

J Mertus, J Tesanovic, H Metikos & R Boric (eds), *The Suitcase: Refugee Voices from Bosnia and Croatia* (University of California Press 1997) p 122.

---

they have already been persecuted, merely that they have good reason to fear persecution. In practice, refugees can find themselves in an almost impossible position: they may not be believed if their story of persecution is highly unusual, yet if it is typical of countless other refugees from their region, they may be suspected of having been schooled in what to say. Hard evidence for their claims is often scant, as many do not have time to gather documentation before they flee and may lack visible scars to corroborate their stories, and they can be judged harshly for failures of memory, even though concentration and memory problems are known consequences of trauma.

Although general practice since World War Two has been to grant refugees permanent residence – indeed they were welcomed in times of labor shortage – since the 1990s some countries have instituted policies of temporary refugee protection. The UNHCR cautiously welcomes such measures if they offer rapid means of accepting large numbers of refugees prior to prompt individual processing for permanent protection. Yet this is rarely the case. 'Temporary' arrangements often leave refugees in an indefinite state of uncertainty, their fear unabated. The drafters of the Refugee Convention were too concerned with the self-interest of receiving countries to guarantee permanent resettlement to all refugees. A country's obligation to protect a refugee ends if 'the circumstances in connection with which he [*sic*] has been recognized as a refugee have ceased to exist.' The Convention does, however, prohibit *refoulement* and obliges states 'as far as possible [to] facilitate the assimilation and naturalization of refugees.' Given that many conflicts last for years – think of Sri Lanka, Timor Leste, Colombia, Northern Ireland, Sudan and Afghanistan – it may be in receiving countries' interests to admit refugees permanently so that they may better establish themselves and contribute to their host society.

Other appealing options for some (Northern) countries include arbitrary limits on their refugee intake (a violation of the Convention) and 'border protection.' Convention obligations cannot be invoked if refugees are prevented from arriving in the first place. This may mean withholding entry visas from 'high-risk' applicants or erecting physical barriers to entry. Australia is particularly notorious in this regard, policing the high seas for leaky fishing vessels (despite the fact that

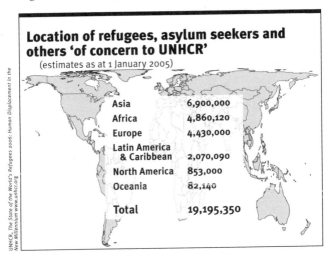

Location of refugees, asylum seekers and others 'of concern to UNHCR'
(estimates as at 1 January 2005)

Asia	6,900,000
Africa	4,860,120
Europe	4,430,000
Latin America & Caribbean	2,070,090
North America	853,000
Oceania	82,140
Total	**19,195,350**

UNHCR, *The State of the World's Refugees 2006: Human Displacement in the New Millennium* www.unhcr.org

most refugees arrive by plane) and detaining some of those intercepted on foreign soil in Papua New Guinea and Nauru. Such reprehensible practices – entirely at odds with the spirit of the Refugee Convention – serve to stigmatize refugees as somehow undesirable and possibly even dangerous (why else would borders need protection?). They also shift the burden of refugee protection to the South, where governments are less able to police their borders. Côte d'Ivoire accepts nearly twice as many refugees as the United States. The leading destination for asylum seekers in 2004 was Iran.

The number of people 'of concern' to the UNHCR rose by about 13 per cent in 2004, from 17 million to 19.2 million (see table). Of these, 47 per cent are children. Only 48 per cent are refugees (and falling). Though not formally responsible for them, UNHCR concerns itself with some of the world's internally displaced persons (IDPs). These are people who flee their home for the same reasons as refugees, but have not crossed a national border. As such, they are not protected by the Refugee Convention. However, in global terms IDPs are twice as numerous as refugees: about 25 million in at least 50 countries (more than half of them in Africa). Like refugees, they are mostly women and children. Aside from the Second Geneva Protocol, which prohibits the displacement of civilian populations, and the non-binding Cartagena Declaration, IDPs are largely ignored by international law. In 1998 the UN issued thirty *Guiding Principles* – reaffirmed by the 2005 World Summit – on how governments and NGOs ought to treat IDPs, emphasizing their human rights.[19]

'…as the number of refugees increased dramatically in recent decades, it has become clear that humanitarian work cannot act as a substitute for political action in avoiding or solving future crises.' ∎
    UNHCR, 'Most frequently asked questions about the Refugee Convention,' *Refugees*, Vol 2, No 123 (July 2001) p 17.

Should human rights be enforced by military means?

Oddly enough, we often use military language in human rights: words like fight, campaign and strategy. But are human rights and military might amenable bedfellows? Two long-standing principles of human rights shed some light on this question.

Human rights are often cast as a natural ally (if you'll forgive the military-speak) not of war but of peace. Certainly both goals are (ideally) foremost at the UN. The UDHR understands the two as intimately connected: human rights are 'the foundation of... peace in the world.' As we have seen, abuses of human rights may be a factor behind conflict, and even non-state terrorism. Armed conflict is certainly a major cause of human rights abuses, especially the right to life, human welfare and property. For example, more than 14 million people worldwide face hunger due to current or recent conflicts. Other grievous abuses associated with modern warfare include the use of child soldiers, the proliferation of small arms, indiscriminate use of landmines and large-scale forced displacement. Given the devastation armed conflict causes, it's hard to see how waging war could possibly aid the cause of human rights.

At the same time there is a tradition in human rights that understands freedom as so important and tyranny so intolerable, that the people have a right to overthrow, by force if necessary, a government that breaches the (implied) social contract (see chapter 1 for more on this). The US *Declaration of Independence* of 1776 puts it this way:

'Whenever any Form of Government becomes destructive of [inalienable rights], it is the Right of the People to alter or to abolish it, and to institute new Government.'

The UDHR echoes this: 'it is essential, if man [*sic*] is not to be compelled to have recourse, as a last resort, to rebellion against tyranny and oppression,

79

that human rights should be protected by the rule of law.' Thus, some would see a proper role for force in the pursuit of human rights.

What if people subject to a despotic government are unable to overthrow their oppressors? What if they call for international assistance? How, in practice, can external actors reliably identify the voice of 'the people' in such circumstances? Can a 'humanitarian intervention' ever be free of vested interests? Why, for example, was Saddam Hussein's presidency intolerable (after all those years), but atrocities in Darfur not equally so? The war on Iraq is hardly a good example of a humanitarian intervention, of course. (We increasingly find human rights goals used to justify wars with far less noble objectives and must contest their misappropriation for such purposes.) The plainest, least-contested example of a situation demanding intervention, both before and during the outbreak of violence, was the 1994 genocide in Rwanda, when the international community failed up to a million people who were killed.

An evolving response to humanitarian crises is the notion of the 'responsibility to protect' (in its hip guise, 'R2P'). It makes sense, when asserting a right to freedom from crimes against humanity and genocide, to tease out who has the responsibility of upholding those rights and how. After such deplorable failures of responsibility as occurred in Rwanda, there has been a growing impetus to establish guidelines for impartial and effec-

'In the humanitarian interventions of the 1990s... Western militaries had spare capacity and time to do human rights work. Now, with America launched on an indefinite military campaign against terrorists, will there be the political energy necessary to mount humanitarian interventions?' ■
Michael Ignatieff, former Professor of Human Rights Policy at Harvard, 'Is the human rights era ending?' *New York Times*, 5 February 2002.

tive humanitarian intervention (see box). Discussions to date have reasserted states' primary responsibility to protect their own people. Where they are unwilling or unable to do so, the international community shares a responsibility to protect civilians. Its response should be non-military initially, then, if necessary, coercive or forceful. Security is thus redefined collectively. There is a growing consensus that a state's sovereign rights are waived if it conducts or permits widespread harm to its own people. In turn, states must not ignore such events occurring in other countries, regardless of their own perceived interests. They must prevent, react and rebuild, as necessary. The UN Secretary-General and a growing number of civil society groups have endorsed R2P.[20] Heads of states meeting at the 2005 World Summit gave it 'clear and unambiguous' support. In coming years, as these principles are implemented (or overlooked), we will be able to judge their contribution to the struggle for human rights.

Should human rights be sacrificed for security?

Former UN High Commissioner for Human Rights Mary Robinson called it 'the T question'[21]: should measures designed to prevent non-state terrorism trump all else? Nearly every government in the world – many of

---

When to intervene?

Responsibility to protect (R2P) guidelines emphasize:
* right cause (a 'supreme humanitarian emergency')
* right intention
* right authority
* last resort
* proportionate means (what degree of force)
* reasonable prospects (high probability of achieving a humanitarian outcome)

International Commission on Intervention and State Sovereignty, *The Responsibility to Protect* (Government of Canada 2001); NJ Wheeler, *Saving Strangers: Humanitarian Intervention in International Society* (Oxford University Press 2000)

---

them already highly repressive – has answered the question by introducing new 'anti-terror' laws and practices, often at the expense of human rights. Typical of such measures are arbitrary detention, often prolonged and incommunicado; the removal of safeguards against torture; unfair trials; loose definitions of 'terrorism' that criminalize the exercise of fundamental freedoms; limitations on the right to freedom of association, labor rights, the right to asylum and freedom from discrimination. This is happening somewhere near you. Here's a handful of examples.

Within weeks of the destruction of the World Trade Center in New York on 11 September 2001, six Zimbabwean journalists had been re-labeled as terrorists. A spokesman for President Mugabe said, 'We agree with US President Bush that anyone who in any way finances, harbors or defends terrorists is himself a terrorist.' Critics of the Government have increasingly been subject to intimidation, harassment and arrest. Calls for a free press in Zimbabwe have been dismissed as a 'mad request, especially in this age of terrorism.'[22]

Syria has boasted of being ahead of the US in fighting terrorism – referring presumably, to Damascus' bloody 25-year campaign against the Islamist resistance organization the Society of the Muslim Brothers – and has invited the US to learn from its example. The Syrian example includes mass arrests, torture with impunity and extra-judicial executions on an immense scale.

Even before the 2005 London bombings, the UK's Labour Government had banned public protests within a kilometer (0.6 of a mile) of the Houses of Parliament

---

'Terrorism is the war of the poor, and war is the terrorism of the rich.'
The late British actor and writer Peter Ustinov, speaking on
German TV in March 2003.

without prior police approval. These laws are incompatible with provisions of the European Convention on Human Rights, such as freedom of assembly and expression. Similar tendencies are evident in other EU countries, including France, Germany and Italy.

Terrorist attacks are a violation of human rights, and governments that fail to take adequate measures to avert and punish such attacks fail in their human rights obligations. And yet human rights, 'no less than counter-terrorism measures, are aimed towards protecting the security of the person.'[23] A commitment to human rights is a commitment to the eradication of state and non-state terrorism. To return to Mary Robinson: before she was forced from her UN post on 11 September 2002 for her criticism of the US's 'war on terror,' she maintained that 'if human rights are respected ... conflict, terrorism and war can be prevented.'[24]

Renewed debate about torture

The questions emerged in public debate shortly after 11 September 2001. Can torture ever be justified? Should it be part of our arsenal in the 'war on terror'? Should certain forms of state torture be sanctioned under certain circumstances?

The ensuing debate (generated, some contend, by the FBI seeking public acceptance for its nefarious plans) is a salutary reminder that the struggle for human rights is never over and we can't afford to take anything for granted. The long-established, widely held human rights position in relation to torture is that it, and related forms of inhuman behavior, are never acceptable. Full stop. The *Convention Against Torture and Other Forms of Cruel, Inhuman or Degrading Treatment or Punishment*, finalized in 1984 and since ratified by 141 countries, makes this clear.

One of the more prominent voices to come out in favor of torture (in limited forms and circumstances) is Harvard academic lawyer Alan Dershowitz. Like others, he relies on the hypothetical 'ticking-bomb' scenario, in which a person who has planted a time-bomb is in custody and only through torture can information necessary to save lives be extracted before the bomb explodes.

This comic-book scenario makes a number of narrow and unlikely assumptions, such as the person

---

Morality and democracy

'Socrates believed that... it is better to suffer evil than to do it... Morality, as Socrates understood it, may require us to renounce the means to achieve what we most passionately believe and decently desire and the means to protect what we rightly cherish.'

R Gaita, 'Breach of Trust: Truth, morality and politics,' *Quarterly Essay 16*, (Black Inc 2004), pp 51-2

'[D]emocracies limit the powers that governments can justly exercise over the human beings under their power, and [these limits should] include an absolute ban on subjecting individuals to forms of pain that strip them of their dignity, identity and even sanity... [T]hose of us who believe this had better admit that many of our fellow citizens are bound to disagree. It is in the nature of democracy itself.' ■

M Ignatieff, 'If torture works...' in K Roth, M Worden & AD Berstein (eds), *Torture: Does it Make Us Safer? Is it Ever OK?: A Human Rights Perspective* (New Press/Human Rights Watch: 2006)

we have in custody is the guilty party and that we can somehow, under time and performance pressures, be certain of this. It also assumes the information we want can't be gained any other way. (Others in the debate have gone further, advocating torturing innocent people – to death if needs be – if they know something.[25]) Putting aside for the moment the fact that no-one has ever been able to cite a real-life situation analogous to the ticking-bomb scenario, the unreliability of torture as a means of gaining correct information, and also the deficits of consequentialist ethics, let's examine a few implications of such a policy were it applied in practice.

To begin with, we would need people who are available, willing and trained to elicit information by torture. In reality trainee torturers are desensitized to the task by being brutalized or tortured themselves.

A torturer's testimony

Jeffrey Benzien (former security policeman): Yes, I did terrible things, I did terrible things to members of the ANC, but as God is my witness, believe me, I have also suffered. I may not call myself a victim of apartheid, but yes Sir, I have also been a victim.

Tony Yengeni (one of his victims): What kind of man uses a method like the wet bag, to people, to other human beings repeatedly and, listening to those moans and cries and groans, takes each of those people very near to their deaths? What kind of man are you? . . . When you do those things, what happens to you as a human being? What goes through your head, your mind? You know, what effect does that torture activity have on you as a human being?

Benzien: Mr Yengeni, not only you have asked me that question. I, I, Jeff Benzien, have asked myself that question to such an extent that I voluntarily – and it is not easy for me to say this in a full court with a lot of people who do not know me – approached psychiatrists to have myself evaluated, to find out what type of person am I. There was a stage when I thought I was losing my mind. I have subsequently been, and I am now still, under treatment. ■

Edited testimony to the South African Truth and Reconciliation Commission regarding the killing of Ashley Kriel and the torture of activists (July 1997). www.doj.gov.za

Often they are also indoctrinated with beliefs about their victims' inhumanity. Both parties are dehumanized. Is it ever reasonable to ask someone to submit to this? Can it be good for a society to create and empower people capable of such inhuman conduct?

Assuming we had torturers at our disposal, what would we ask them to do? Professor Dershowitz suggests sterilized needles inserted under the fingernails as a non-lethal form of torture that would cause 'unbearable pain' (his words) but no lasting harm. Frankly, this is plain ignorant. Whatever torture's effect on different people, it is more than physical, always lasting and often permanent. So-called 'torture lite' (prolonged standing, hooding, sleep deprivation and the like) is no more acceptable (see box on p 87). Nice of him to think of sterilizing the needles, though.

What coercive techniques should be sanctioned? How would they be institutionalized? Should doctors be present to ensure the torture remains within non-lethal bounds? To do so would be a gross contravention of medical ethics. Philosopher Raimond Gaita cautions us about (at least) one slippery slope: 'If there is moral pressure to torture one person to a limited degree to save the lives of many, why is there not much the same pressure to exceed those limits if he doesn't talk?'[26] Policy based on the worst-possible scenario

---

Not in my name

'If a person fully understood what he was doing, had it vividly before his mind, could he consent to the torture of someone for his sake? Only someone who lived as though every principle is negotiable when his life is at risk. Such a life is not worthy of a human being... These, I admit, are not truths written in the heavens. Neither facts nor reason compel their acceptance. But the finest part of our tradition has taught them and many have given their lives rather than betray them. Before democracy, even before freedom, it is for them that we should fight.' ■

R Gaita, 'Breach of Trust: Truth, morality and politics,' *Quarterly Essay 16* (Black Inc 2005) pp 51-2.

Lasting cruelty

'Sleep deprivation leads to cognitive impairment, including attention deficits and impaired memory, reasoning, verbal communication and decision-making. The effects of prolonged isolation can be especially devastating and can include an inability to think or concentrate, disorientation, hallucinations, depression and other severe mental health problems, including self-harm and attempted suicide.'

Amnesty International, 'Torture and ill-treatment: The arguments' (London). web.amnesty.org

What it's like

Psychotherapist John Schlapobersky describes the impact of the torture he himself suffered as a student activist in South Africa, being forced to stand and stay awake for five days from Friday to Wednesday, broken only by one period of rest on Monday night:

'[I]t was a very strange state of wakefulness, because by Sunday I was hallucinating and I didn't really know where I was... who they were. I didn't know the time of day... I didn't have a sense of place... ... I think my own sense of fighting them became much less obvious by Saturday night. Sunday, my feet swelled up... I was in a lot of pain... On the Monday, I can remember walking into walls. I would start walking in this tiny room, dashing into the wall and wake up with a terrible fright and hurt my face. And I can remember them... little clusters of them standing at the door... laughing at my confusion. On the Monday night, not only my feet were swollen, but also I was very edematous in my thighs... I think it was Tuesday morning that they woke me. I was more confused than at any other point. I wasn't sure if I was dreaming or awake... I was slightly crazy.' ∎

H Bernstein, *The Rift: The Exile Experience of South Africans* (Jonathan Cape 1994) pp 83-5.

is notoriously flawed and open to abuse. There's no doubt that torture sanctioned for exclusively 'ticking-bomb' purposes would get out of control.

Whatever the outcome of the current debate, it remains a fact that torture does occur, formally sanctioned or not, in over 150 countries throughout the world. To suggest that its prevalence is a reason to legalize torture is naïve, not to say defeatist. Torture is used for reasons far beyond information gathering; to legalize it for 'ticking-bomb' interrogations would not restrain other uses. Watering down the absolute ban

Rights in war and armed conflict

legitimizes torture. Torture can be stamped out.[27] If the reality of torture is 'vividly before our mind,' there can be no other way.

1 H Dunant, *A Memory of Solferino* (Cassell 1947; originally published in 1862). **2** A Roberts & R Guelff (eds), *Documents on the Laws of War*, 3rd edn (Oxford University Press 2000) p 53. **3** International Committee of the Red Cross, *International Humanitarian Law: Answers to your Questions* (2002), p 9. **4** Genesis 18:20-33. **5** Art. 35(2) First Additional Protocol to the Geneva Conventions. **6** See common articles 1, 2 and 3. **7** International Committee of the Red Cross, 'Basic rules of international humanitarian law in armed conflicts'(1988) www.icrc.org **8** R Overy, 'The Nuremberg Trials: International Law in the Making' in P Sands (ed) *From Nuremberg to the Hague: The Future of International Criminal Justice* (Cambridge University Press 2003) pp 3-4. **9** Art. 46 of the 1st Geneva Convention, Art. 47 of the 2nd Geneva Convention, Art. 27 and 33 of the 4th Geneva Convention, Art. 20, 75(2) & 76 of the 1st Geneva Protocol & Art. 4(2) of the 2nd Geneva Protocol. **10** Art. 7(1g) of the Rome Statute. Rape was also defined as a crime against humanity in the statues of the ICTY (Art. 5g) and the ICTR (Art. 3g). **11** J Mertus, 'Shouting from the bottom of the well: The impact of international trials for wartime rape on women's agency' in P Gready (ed.), *Political Transition: Politics and Cultures* (Pluto Press 2003). **12** A Clapham, 'Issues of complexity, complicity and complementarity: From the Nuremberg trials to the dawn of the new International Criminal Court' in P Sands (ed), *From Nuremberg to the Hague: The Future of International Criminal Justice* (Cambridge University Press 2003), p 49. **13** D Petrasek & P Hicks, *Hard Cases: Bringing Human Rights Violators to Justice Abroad: A Guide to Universal Jurisdiction* (International Council on Human Rights Policy 1999). **14** P Sands, *Lawless World: America and the Making and Breaking of Global Rules* (Allen Lane 2005) pp 216-17. **15** Amnesty International, *Gacaca: A question of justice* (2002). http://web.amnesty.org **16** G Galant & M Parlevliet, 'Using rights to address conflict: A valuable synergy' in P Gready & J Ensor (eds), *Reinventing Development? Translating Rights-Based Approaches from Theory into Practice* (Zed Books 2005). **17** Art. 1(2) of the *Convention Governing the Specific Aspects of Refugee Problems in Africa*. **18** UNHCR, 'Protecting Refugees' www.unhcr.ch **19** UN Office for the Coordination of Humanitarian Affairs, *Guiding Principles on Internal Displacement* (1998) www.idpproject.org **20** www.responsibility-toprotect.org **21** S Vieira de Mello, 'Five questions for the human rights field' in *Sur International Journal on Human Rights* No 1 (2004) pp 165-71, www.surjournal.org **22** HRW, 'Opportunism in the Face of Tragedy: Repression in the name of anti-terrorism' www.hrw.org **23** Joint Declaration on the Need for an International Mechanism to Monitor Human Rights and Counter-Terrorism adopted at the ICJ Conference of 23-25 October 2003 in Geneva. **24** Editorial, 'Mary Robinson: Human Rights Crusader,' *The Boston Globe* (3 September 2002). **25** M Bagaric & J Clarke, 'Not Enough (Official) Torture In The World: The circumstances in which torture is morally justifiable', *University of San Francisco Law Review*, 39 (2005) pp 1-39. **26** R Gaita, 'Breach of trust: Truth, morality and politics,' *Quarterly Essay 16* (2005) p 55. **27** See, for example, *Combating Torture: A Manual for Action* (Amnesty International 2003), available in English, French and Spanish, and the Optional Protocol to the Convention Against Torture (2002).

4 Law and what it's good for

Roosevelt and Churchill met on a ship during World War Two and drew up a single-page document that became the basis of modern international law. The principles contained in the Atlantic Charter, including human rights, peace and disarmament, would later reaffirm Nelson Mandela's faith in humanity.[1] National and international human rights law have come a long way since then.

INTERNATIONAL LAW IS an essential part of our globalized world. Its usually smooth operation makes its pervasive presence invisible in our daily lives: governing airspace and the high seas, trade and economic relations, international organizations and communications, diplomatic relations and environmental issues, and the settlement of disputes between nations. International law sets minimum standards of behavior that seek to obviate international bullying and military action. In this respect it is a mechanism to promote justice and peace as much as orderliness and predictability in the conduct of international affairs.

Certainly, international law is not all noble sentiment: it is a means by which countries seek to promote their interests. But, increasingly, governments find that it is in their interests to participate in international legal institutions and adhere to their laws. Though some countries endeavor to opt out of some treaties, such as the US and Australia's shunning of the Kyoto Protocol on climate change, they may find that selfish uncooperativeness is not, in fact, in their long-term interests. International lawyer Philippe Sands argues that private industries incurring the costs of reducing their carbon dioxide emissions will exert pressure on Kyoto-compliant governments to impose trade restrictions on those non-compliant nations that can produce and export cheaper goods by abusing the

> 'There is a difference between arbitrary power and the rule of law. We ought to expose the shams and inequities which may be concealed beneath this law. But the rule of law itself... seems to me to be an unqualified human good... We feel contempt not because we are contemptuous of the notion of a just and equitable law, but because this notion has been betrayed by its own professors.' ■
> EP Thompson, *Whigs and Hunters: The Origin of the Black Act* (Pantheon Books 1975) pp 266-8.

environment.[2] In this interdependent world, it is in all states' (and often all people's) long-term interests that international law is obeyed.

Historically, international law is shifting from serving exclusively the interests of states to, in the post-World War Two era, serving the interests of people (and corporations) as well. The means by which international law is created and adopted has yet to catch up. Most international treaties are not debated adequately, if at all, in national parliaments. This lack of democratic input into international law is certainly one of its failings, but not one that cannot be corrected. There is a growing popular appreciation of how international law affects us on the ground and a corresponding interest in having a say in it. The 'Battle of Seattle' in 1999 and similar protests are testimony to this. The war on Iraq and related events generated worldwide public interest in international law.

Although public consultation may be limited at the time of ratification, human rights treaties are inevitably the product of extensive, concerted struggle by social movements. In the 1940s, it was NGOs that ensured inclusion of human rights in the UN Charter and contributed to the UDHR.[3] The 1984 Torture Convention began as a transnational campaign targeting torture by the military regime in Greece. NGOs had an unprecedented role in the drafting of the *Convention on the Rights of the Child*.[4] Transnational human rights campaigns and international

> 'In the absence of sustained campaigns and lobbying efforts by INGOs and particular individuals, probably not a single human right would have been written into international law.' ■
>
> T Risse, 'The power of norms versus the norms of power: transnational civil society and human rights', in AM Florini (ed.), *The Third Force: The Rise of Transnational Civil Society* (Japan Center for International Exchange 2000) p 184.

norms have a mutually enforcing relationship.

International law takes a number of different forms. There are treaties, often called covenants, conventions or protocols, which are signed and ratified by individual countries, and are then legally binding upon those countries (even after changes of government). There are also non-binding international agreements on human rights, often in the form of declarations or recommendations, on which large numbers of countries agree, but are more like authoritative guidelines intended to inform policy and practice rather than legal obligations. These are often dubbed 'soft law', while treaties are said to be 'hard law'.

There is also customary international law. These laws are not negotiated or enacted, but exist as precedents in the way things have been done in the past. Whether such law exists may be a matter of dispute until a court says that it does or, perhaps, overwhelming expert opinion agrees that it does. Custom often forms the basis of international treaties.

The most pertinent customary international law for our purposes is the UDHR. Although it was originally declared in 1948 as a non-binding form of 'soft law' (and therefore has no signatories), its standing over the years has grown to such an extent that it now has customary law status.[5] As such, it is binding on all states as international law. What can such a strange assertion mean, in a world full of human rights violations?

The fact is most international law cannot be enforced in the same way that national (or 'domestic') law can be enforced. Transgressors – whether individuals, governments, corporations or other collective bodies, both private and public – are not usually arrested, tried and punished (with exceptions discussed in chapter 3). In most cases, short of using military force, countries must be shamed, persuaded and pressured into making and abiding by commitments to international human rights norms. Ultimately, law enforcement, like law making, cannot be divorced from politics (see chapter 5).

UN treaties

'Human rights are inscribed in the hearts of people; they were there long before lawmakers drafted their first proclamation.' ∎
Mary Robinson, former UN High Commissioner for Human Rights.

Following the adoption of the UDHR in 1948, international efforts focused on the development and ratification of legally-binding human rights instruments (see chapter 2). We now have seven major covenants expressing an almost universal, comprehensive understanding of what 'human rights' are – the most credible expression yet of a global human ethic, expressed in political and legal terms – to which most countries of the world have committed themselves (see table).

One might add the 1948 *Convention on the Prevention and Punishment of the Crime of Genocide* with its 133 state parties, or any number of other human rights 'instruments'. They can be found at the website of the Office of the High Commissioner for Human Rights (www.ohchr.org).

Treaties are usually negotiated over a long period and invariably involve compromises, even inconsistencies. For example, the *Convention on the Rights of the Child* defines a child as being under 18 years of age, but allows children as young as 15 to perform active military service. A decade later an optional protocol raised

Seven key human rights treaties

Year adopted	Full title and acronym	Number of countries bound by the treaty*
1966	International Covenant on Economic, Social and Cultural Rights (ICESCR)	153
1966	International Covenant on Civil and Political Rights (ICCPR)	156
1966	International Convention on the Elimination of All Forms of Racial Discrimination (CERD)	170
1979	Convention on the Elimination of All Forms of Discrimination Against Women (CEDAW)	182
1984	Convention Against Torture and other Cruel, Inhuman or Degrading Treatment or Punishment (CAT)	141
1989	Convention on the Rights of the Child (CRC)	192
1990	International Convention on the Protection of the Rights of All Migrant Workers and Members of their Families (ICRMW)	34

* as at 10 April 2006.

Office of the UN High Commissioner for Human Rights, 'Status of Ratifications of the Principal International Human Rights Treaties' www.ohchr.org

the age to 18. Once adopted, governments are invited to sign and ratify the treaty. Signing a treaty indicates a state's support for the treaty and intent to ratify, perhaps after consulting further or amending national laws. Ratification is the goal, however, at which point a state is legally bound to implement the treaty.

Even at this point, there is a means by which governments may opt out of specific provisions of the treaty in advance: by entering a formal 'reservation' stating what part of the treaty they will not be bound by and why (although reservations should not undermine the 'object and purpose' of the treaty[6]). The treaty is said to 'enter into force,' or become binding, once a specified number of countries have ratified it. The ICCPR and ICESCR, for example, were adopted and opened

Looking for more detail?

Expressed in a mere line or two in the UDHR, there's a shelf-full of books on how to interpret each human right, based on subsequent declarations, international agreements and expert opinions issued by the UN and others, as well as binding treaties and legal precedent. By way of example, here are some of the international human rights instruments dealing with the right to education:

Universal Declaration of Human Rights (1948)
Convention relating to the Status of Refugees (1951)
Declaration of the Rights of the Child (1959)
Convention Against Discrimination in Education (UNESCO, 1960)
International Covenant on Economic, Social and Cultural Rights (1966)
Declaration on the Rights of Disabled Persons (1975)
Recommendation on the Development of Adult Education (UNESCO, 1976)
International Charter of Physical Education and Sport (UNESCO, 1978)
Limburg Principles on the Implementation of the International Covenant on Economic, Social and Cultural Rights (1986)
Convention (No 169) Concerning Indigenous and Tribal Peoples in Independent Countries (ILO 1989)
Convention on Technical and Vocational Education (UNESCO, 1989)
Convention on the Rights of the Child (1989)
World Declaration on Education for All (1990)
Cairo Declaration on Human Rights in Islam (1990)
International Convention on the Protection of the Rights of All Migrant Workers and Members of Their Families (1990)
Declaration on the Rights of Persons Belonging to National or Ethnic, Religious and Linguistic Minorities (1992)
Vienna Declaration and Programme of Action (1993)
Standard Rules on the Equalization of Opportunities for Persons with Disabilities (1993)
Draft Declaration on the Rights of Indigenous Peoples (1994)
Plan of Action for the United Nations Decade for Human Rights Education (1994)
Recommendation Concerning the Status of Higher-Education Teaching Personnel (UNESCO, 1997)
Maastricht Guidelines on Violations of Economic, Social and Cultural Rights (1997)
CESCR General Comment 13: The right to education (1999)
        D Hodgson, The Human Right to Education (Aldershot 1998).

for signature in 1966, but did not attract enough ratifications to enter into force until 1976.

All this has occurred since World War Two and is continuing. Potential new legal norms now in development include a Declaration on the Rights of Indigenous Peoples, a Declaration on the Right to Water, an International Convention on the Protection of All Persons from Forced Disappearance and a Comprehensive and Integral Convention to promote and protect the Rights and Dignity of Persons with Disabilities.

Can or should legal rights be expanded indefinitely? In the opinion of former UN High Commissioner for Human Rights, the late Sergio Vieira de Mello, 'there can only be so many categories of human rights to be found in the world... I suspect, obviously, that there are still other categories to areas to be discovered... Yet there is a limit to the expansion of these different types or categories of rights, as there is a limit also to the proliferation of treaties and mechanisms and special procedures.'[7] His predecessor Mary Robinson agreed in 1999 that: 'During the past decade the emphasis has shifted from standard-setting to improving the implementation of human rights.'[8]

UN bodies

Without ongoing attention, monitoring and enforcement, treaties, once agreed, risk being forgotten, empty documents of mere historical interest. Human rights obligations need to be kept alive by continually reminding duty-holders of their shortcomings. NGOs have a clear role here, both in UN fora and elsewhere, while some treaties have their own monitoring bodies.

Each of the seven human rights treaties listed has an associated committee composed of independent experts with ultimate authority to interpret the treaty. The Committee on Economic, Social and Cultural Rights, for example, monitors the ICESCR, and so on. Rather confusingly, the people monitoring the ICCPR are called the Human Rights Committee. These committees issue statements (known as 'General Comments') on the meaning and correct implementation of their treaty. Additional functions of the committees vary: some receive periodic reports from ratifying countries (frequently submitted late) and, increasingly, 'shadow reports' submitted by civil society. They may question state representatives and publish views ('Concluding Observations') on that state's compliance. Some are empowered to receive individual complaints (or 'communications') alleging state violations of the treaty and make quasi-judicial decisions about them. Some can also receive complaints by one state party against another, but, in practice, this never happens.

Most international mechanisms require complainants to have exhausted all domestic remedies first (where they are genuine rather than illusory[9]). Domestic avenues may be quicker and more effective anyway. For details on how to submit a complaint to the UN go to: www.ohchr.org/english/bodies/petitions/index.htm

Human Rights Committee – oversees the ICCPR, issuing general comments (31 so far), receiving state reports about every four years and passing judgement on any individual complaints against those countries that have ratified the 1st Optional Protocol to the ICCPR.

Committee on Economic, Social and Cultural Rights – monitors the ICESCR, making general comments (18 so far) and proceeds with periodic state reviews, even if the country in question fails to submit a report. It does not yet have the power to receive individual complaints, although an optional protocol is in development. Expert opinion on states' obligations in regard to economic, social and cultural rights is also found in the 1986 Limburg Principles and 1997 Maastricht Guidelines.

Committee on the Elimination of Racial Discrimination – monitors CERD, conducting country reviews every couple of years (even in the absence of a state submission) and issuing general recommendations (31 so far) and thematic discussion papers. It can receive individual complaints (according to Article 14 of CERD, rather than a separate protocol). This committee also has an early-warning system to try to prevent serious violations of the Convention. Recent warnings have concerned Israel, Darfur, Laos, Suriname and Aotearoa/New Zealand.

Committee on the Elimination of Discrimination Against Women – receives and comments on states' reports on their implementation of CEDAW every four years. Individual complaints may be made against those states that are also party to the 1999 Optional Protocol.

Committee Against Torture – issues general comments in relation to CAT (only one so far) and receives and comments on state reports every four years. It will also receive individual communications if the accused state has consented to Article 22. Committee members may visit countries suspected of systematic torture, with that state's consent. A 2002 Optional Protocol to the Convention establishes national and international monitoring bodies that also visit places of detention.

Committee on the Rights of the Child – monitors the CRC and its two Optional Protocols that deal with the rights of children in relation to armed conflict (OP-CRC-AC) and trafficking, prostitution and pornography (OP-CRC-SC), respectively. State parties are expected to report every five years to the Committee, which then makes concluding observations as well as general comments (seven so far). It is not empowered to receive individual complaints.

Committee on Migrant Workers – held its first annual meeting in 2004 to monitor the ICRMW. It examines

---

Alternative or 'shadow' reports to the Committee on the Rights of the Child

A network of child rights NGOs consulted nearly a thousand children in order to compile a shadow report as an alternative to Uganda's first periodic report to the Committee on the Rights of the Child in 2005. The process of preparing the report gave these organizations a better understanding of the reporting process, and of how to effect change and use information to promote child well-being. They found it to be a way of influencing policy and holding decision-makers accountable. Shadow reports submitted to the Committee on the Rights of the Child are available at: www.crin.org ∎

Ugandan Child Rights NGO Network report 'shadowing' Uganda's First Periodic Report to the Committee on the Rights of the Child, 40th Session, September 2005.

---

states' reports every five years, and issues concluding observations and general comments. It will also receive complaints of specific violations (communications) once ten states parties allow it.

In contrast with these seven committees – known collectively as 'treaty-based bodies' because they are established by their associated treaty – is a Charter-based body (established by the 1945 UN Charter), which ranks alongside the Security Council, namely the Human Rights Council (not to be confused with the Commission on Human Rights, which it replaced in 2006, or the Human Rights Committee, described above). Of the UN's 191 member states, 47 sit on this Council, elected by simple majority of the General Assembly in a secret ballot. Geographically diverse, they serve a maximum of six years and may have their membership suspended for gross human rights violations. The Geneva-based Council meets at least three times a year, in addition to special sessions convened to respond to urgent situations. Like the Commission on Human Rights before it, the Council has independent experts (rapporteurs) who receive communications (complaints), undertake fact-finding missions

Some bits of the UN

A partial diagram as at 2006 – note that the 2005 World Summit replaced the Commission on Human Rights with the Human Rights Council, approved the creation of a Peacebuilding Commission to support post-conflict peacebuilding and recovery and added a standing police force to UN peacekeeping.

Security Council	Human Rights Council	General Assembly	ECOSOC (Economic and Social Council)
peacekeeping		Children's Fund (UNICEF)	World Bank Group
		Development Program (UNDP)	International Monetary Fund (IMF)
International Criminal Tribunal for the former Yugoslavia (ICTY)		Environment Program (UNEP)	Commission on the Status of Women
International Criminal Tribunal for Rwanda (ICTR)		Development Fund for Women (UNIFEM)	Permanent Forum on Indigenous Issues
		Population Fund (UNFPA)	World Health Organization (WHO)
		Human Settlements Program (UN-HABITAT)	International Labour Organization (ILO)
		World Food Program (WFP)	
		High Commissioner for Refugees (UNHCR)	Food and Agriculture Organization (FAO)
		High Commissioner for Human Rights (OHCHR)	Educational, Scientific & Cultural Organization (UNESCO)

and write reports.

As Secretary-General, Kofi Annan sought to 'mainstream' rights throughout the UN. Most, if not all, arms of the organization have an impact on human rights, at times a negative impact. UNESCO, for example, promotes universal education, cultural development, press freedom and protection of the world's natural and cultural heritage, while the World Bank's development projects and the 'conditionalities' it imposes on debtor nations often undermine human rights. The highest UN official with responsibility for human rights is the High Commissioner for Human Rights, a post created as late as 1993 and currently held by Canadian Louise Arbour. In 2005 the UN World Summit agreed to double her budget and approved closer co-operation between her office and the rest of the UN.

Regional treaties and courts

Countries with a sense of regional affinity have grouped together to form their own human rights structures, namely the African Union (AU), OAS and the Council of Europe. The Asia-Pacific region (including the Middle East[10]) is not yet at the same point, leaving about two-thirds of the world's population without this stratum of human rights enforcement.

Europe – The 1953 *European Convention on Human Rights* has 13 additional protocols, one of which abolished the European Commission on Human Rights in 1998 and made its parallel Court a full-time feature of a riverbank in Strasbourg, north-eastern France. Individuals, states and NGOs may bring cases of actual or potential violations by any of the 45 participating states. The Court received 13,858 such applications in 2001 alone and has trouble keeping up. Its decisions, including orders to pay compensation to victims, are legally binding. The Committee of Ministers of the Council of Europe is

Pre-emptive use of lethal force

Dan McCann, Mairead Farrell and Sean Savage, three known members of the Provisional IRA believed to be planning a bomb attack, were killed by UK Special Forces in Gibraltar. It was subsequently discovered that they had been unarmed, had no bomb and no detonator. Family members brought a case to the European Court of Human Rights.

The Court accepted that on the basis of flawed intelligence, the soldiers believed there were immediate dangers obliging them to shoot and shoot to kill, but found that the use of lethal force was disproportionate to the threat posed. Nor was it 'absolutely necessary' in that there were other ways the bomb attack might have been prevented. Besides, killing in order to prevent future violence was not deemed an acceptable exception to the right to life. The soldiers were not held individually responsible: the State was responsible for giving them faulty information.

This 1995 case had eerie relevance 10 years later in the lethal shooting of innocent Brazilian Jean Charles de Menezes on a London train. Plainclothes police mistook him for a suspect in the previous day's failed bomb attacks on the London Underground and put seven bullets in his head. Police Commissioner, Ian Blair, claimed the shoot-to-kill policy 'appeared to be the least-worst option' for tackling suicide bombers. ■

McCann and Others v the United Kingdom, ECHR judgement of 27 September 1995 (17/1994/464/545); Australian Broadcasting Corporation News Online, 'UK's shoot-to-kill policy to stay' (21 August 2005) www.abc.net.au

responsible to ensure compliance.

Americas – The Inter-American Court of Human Rights (IACHR) has sat in San José, Costa Rica, since 1979 and now has 25 member states. The American Convention on Human Rights was adopted 10 years earlier. An associated Commission in Washington, DC, receives communications (from individuals, NGOs and states) and determines their admissibility. It also does fact-finding and country visits and may, of its own initiative, investigate and report publicly on the general human rights situation in any OAS member state. Although the US hosts the Commission, it has not ratified the Convention.

Duty to prevent and respond to violations

In 1981, 35-year-old university student Manfredo Velásquez Rodríguez was arrested without warrant in a Honduran car-park in broad daylight. Accused of 'political crimes', he was interrogated and tortured in police custody, although police and security forces denied knowledge of his arrest or whereabouts. His family petitioned the IACHR, believing him to be alive and in prison.

The Court heard evidence concerning Velásquez and over 100 other people who were disappeared and tortured in Honduras between 1981 and 1984. Amnesty and other NGOs acted as *amici curiae* (friends of the court). Some witnesses to the case were murdered. The Court found that Manfredo Velásquez and many others had been kidnapped, tortured, executed and clandestinely buried by the Armed Forces of Honduras, which then took steps to conceal its crimes. Forced disappearance was declared a 'continuous violation of many rights under the [American] Convention,' and systematic disappearances a crime against humanity, intended not only to eliminate those who disappeared, but also to create 'a general state of anguish, insecurity and fear.'

That perpetrators may have acted without direct order or the direct knowledge of their superiors was deemed irrelevant. Further, the State was held responsible for violations committed by private or unidentified actors because of 'the lack of due diligence to prevent the violation or to respond to it... [T]hose parties are aided in a sense by the government, thereby making the State responsible... The existence of a particular violation does not, in itself, prove the failure to take preventive measures, [but] this duty to prevent includes all those means of a legal, political, administrative and cultural nature that promote the protection of human rights and ensure that any violations are considered and treated as illegal acts, which, as such, may lead to the punishment of those responsible.'

The Court ordered Honduras to compensate Velásquez Rodríguez's widow and children materially and to perform other acts of 'moral reparation'. The notion of 'due diligence' established in this case has been used to crystallize State responsibility more generally in relation to the actions of private actors and the private sphere. ■

Africa – The African Charter on Human and Peoples' Rights, adopted by the AU (then the OAU) in 1981, enshrines mutual duties as well as human rights; including duties to family, society and nation, duties to pay taxes, preserve 'positive African cultural values' and promote African unity. It also protects the right to peace and a 'satisfactory environment'. A Commission of 11 experts, meeting on Banjul Island in the mouth of the Gambia River, interprets the Charter, receives periodic state reports and considers individual complaints. Sixteen of the 53 nations in the AU have ratified a protocol establishing an African Court on Human and Peoples' Rights, intended to merge with the AU Court of Justice, and destined to be located in eastern Africa. Its first 11 judges were elected in 2006.

Asia – In the absence of intergovernmental consensus in the Asia-Pacific region, a coalition of NGOs declared 'a people's charter' in 1998 under the auspices of the Asian Human Rights Commission in Hong Kong. The Asian Human Rights Charter incorporates rights to which most Asian states are already committed in existing treaties (such as children's rights), as well as rights less popular with Asian (and other) governments (eg democratic and indigenous rights and the rights of people with disabilities or HIV). Not binding in itself, it is a basis for dialog, a lobbying tool, and a counter-point to claims that Asian values are antithetical to human rights.

Domestic law

Long before the UN or regional treaties, human rights found expression in national constitutions as diverse as the United States of America (1789) and the Kingdom of Tonga in the South Pacific (1875). Governments signing up to an international treaty are supposed to give effect to the provisions of that treaty in national or 'domestic' law so that they become part of national practice and can be applied in national courts. Today, the gold standard in constitutional human rights protection is South Africa's 1996 Bill of Rights. It enshrines economic rights such as food and water and prohibits, amongst other things, discrimination on the grounds of sexual orientation.

Finding shelter in the constitution

In 1986 Olga Tellis and other homeless people in Mumbai used the right to life provision in the Indian Constitution to contest their eviction by the municipality. The High Court found that, in the absence of suitable alternative accommodation, eviction from pavement space close to their place of work deprived them of the means of making a living and, consequently, violated their right to life: 'it would be sheer pedantry to exclude the right to livelihood from the content of the right to life.'

Unlike its Indian counterpart, the South African Constitution explicitly protects the right to housing. In 1999 Irene Grootboom and some 900 other squatters, mostly children, were evicted from private land in Oostenberg Municipality and their improvised shelters destroyed. They went to court, not to contest the legality of their eviction, but to demand the State provide temporary shelter while they sought permanent accommodation. This landmark case drew on international human rights treaties and CESCR General Comments to help interpret the Constitution. It enforced the positive obligation on states to realize progressively rights within available resources and to fulfill immediately certain unqualified rights regardless of budgetary limitations. Best-fit public policy is not good enough if it fails to address the rights of those in most urgent need. The municipal, provincial and national governments were ordered to provide basic shelter, water and sanitation for children who are literally homeless and their parents. The precedent has been invoked by survivors of the 2004 Indian Ocean tsunami. ∎

Olga Tellis v Bombay Municipal Corporation [aka *Bombay Pavement Dwellers Case*] (1986) AIR (SC) 180, p 194; *Grootboom and others v Oostenberg Municipality and others* 2000 (3) BCLR 277(C) at 293A.

Alternatives to constitutional reform include passing statutory legislation protecting human rights. Such legislation is easier to amend than 'entrenched' (constitutional) rights, which can be a plus or a minus. Australia's Constitution is notoriously difficult to change. The US only has a Bill of Rights because its Constitution was subject to amendment. The UK, on the other hand, with its common law tradition, has passed the *Human Rights Act 1998* to 'give further effect' at national level to its regional human rights obligations. As an ordinary act of Parliament, it may be amended by Parliament.

> ## Innocent man may be imprisoned for ever
>
> Ahmed Ali Al-Kateb is a stateless Palestinian born in Kuwait. Having failed to gain refugee status in Australia, he was held in a detention camp while Australia tried to find a country that would accept him. After more than two years in detention and with his migration case going nowhere, Al-Kateb challenged the lawfulness of his detention. His case eventually reached the highest court in Australia. Unconstrained by a bill of rights, the High Court held that, although there was no likelihood that Al-Kateb or others like him would be deported in the foreseeable future, they could be detained indefinitely. ■
>
> *Al-Kateb v Godwin* [2004] HCA 37; *Minister for Immigration v Al Khafaji* [2004] HCA 38.

Legal pluralism

Legal pluralism exists when more than one legal system applies within a state or political unit. The UK, Canada and many other federations and political hierarchies illustrate legal pluralism in action. For many people across the globe it is not state law, still less international law, that are salient: their daily lives are more intimately governed by what is often termed customary law (as distinct from customary *international* law described at the beginning of this chapter). Social norms frequently perform the same regulatory functions as legal norms. This kind of customary law usually differs from human rights law in key respects. It is often oral rather than written; instead of substantive rules and retribution, priority is given to dispute resolution, consensus, compromise and social order; and the group is more important than the individual. A plural system may embody dissonant values, with local customary law reflecting social and cultural mores that may, for example, discriminate against women. Customary law raises important questions about the role of cultural relativism, the reach, capacity and role of the state, and relationships between the local, national and global.

Human rights law does tend to tame rights and

Customary law in a Botswanan village

'People brought to *kgotla* (community council) are not necessarily criminals as we think of it in a court of law. They are brought there by people who want their grievances addressed. These grievances arise over the sharing of property between relatives, the use of impolite words to somebody, a loan of money to somebody who is taking a long time to repay the loan or trespassing on a man's home or land... All we old men sit near the chief and people who have complaints state their case. Our opinion is then asked for by the chief... Then the chief bases his judgement of a case on the views of all present and the complaints are redressed with a fine or some strong words from all present.' ■

Lekoto Digate, an 86-year-old retired cattleman.
B Head, *Serowe: Village of the Rain Wind* (Heinemann 1981) pp 40-1.

---

present them as non-controversial technicalities which, as we have seen, is far from the case. The justicability debate (outlined in chapter 2) gives the misleading impression that only legal rights are 'real,' while rights without force of law are somehow less legitimate. Rights precede law. In the next chapter we shall look at other ways of recognizing and securing human rights.

1 N Mandela, *Long Walk to Freedom: The Autobiography of Nelson Mandela* (Little, Brown & Co. 1994) pp 83-4. **2** P Sands, Alumni Lecture 2005 'Lawless World: International Law after 9/11 and Iraq,' Melbourne Law School (Melbourne, 15 June 2005). **3** W Korey, *NGOs and the Universal Declaration of Human Rights: 'A Curious Grapevine'* (St Martin's Press 1998) ch 1. **4** JE Doek & N Cantwell, *The United Nations Convention on the Rights of the Child: A Guide to the 'Travaux preparatoires'* (Dordrecht 1992). **5** J Humphrey 'The International Bill of Rights: Scope and Implementation,' 17 *William & Mary Law Review* (1976) p 527. **6** Art. 19, *Vienna Convention on the Law of Treaties* (1969). **7** S Vieira de Mello, 'Five questions for the human rights field', in *Sur International Journal on Human Rights* No 1, 2004, pp 165-71, www.surjournal.org/eng **8** M Robinson, 'Constructing an International Financial, Trade and Development Architecture: the Human Rights Dimension', lecture given at the Swiss Federal Institute of Technology, Zurich (1 July 1999). **9** H Hannum, *Guide to International Human Rights Practice*, 3rd edn (Transnational 1999) p 26. **10** The Arab Charter on Human Rights establishes a monitoring body to which states must submit periodic reports. The Charter was adopted in 1994 by the 22-member League of Arab States, but has yet to attract enough ratifications to enter into force.

5 Other ways of securing human rights

Law is not the only, or even the most important, means to assert rights and seek redress for their violation. Ombudsmen, truth commissions and national human rights institutions have a role, as do the diverse activities of civil society.

LEGAL PROCESSES CAN be expensive and slow, unenforced or unenforceable and may be inaccessible to or prejudiced against marginalized groups. Laws, even just laws, are only part of the answer, because law-making and enforcement are a site of ongoing political struggle.

In India, for example, public interest litigation achieved a 2001 Supreme Court 'interim order' that state governments provide cooked lunches in all primary schools within six months. It took a few years to reach 50 million children – easily the largest nutrition program in the world – and it's expanding. Belgian-Indian economist Jean Drèze estimates that 'with adequate public pressure, another 50 million children are likely to get on board within a year or so... The steady progress of midday meals reflects [the] effective combination of legal action and social action.'[1]

British academic Neil Stammers argues that institutionalizing human rights as legal rights could actually be counter-productive: it is in their pre-institutionalized, non-legal form that human rights are most likely to challenge relations and structures of power.[2] Legal efforts ought not to come at the expense of structural reform and attention to underlying, systemic causes of rights violations.

A politics of human rights

The pursuit of human rights is a political project. Prosecution of the 'war on terror', for example, may be illegal and challenged as such, but providing a coherent alternative and pressing for its adoption will require far more than legal acumen. But what kind of politics can human rights support?

Humanitarian worker Paul O'Brien makes the useful distinction between capital-P 'Politics' and lower-case-p 'politics'. The former is partisan, promotes particular political actors or allies, and non-consensual values (eg 'P'oliticized aid in Afghanistan promotes particular actors and US interests); whereas the latter is informed by certain core, higher, consensual or universal political values and takes sides to the extent that it is pro-poor. Human rights are necessarily 'political' because they inform how resources and power are allocated and used.[3]

To be effective, human rights defenders need to embrace a 'principled politics'. Rather than imagining we can or should be non-political, an informed, thought-through political strategy is an invaluable asset. A politics of human rights should emphasize both empowerment and accountability, insist on the full range of rights, acknowledge the rights of all parties while siding with the victims, adjudicate conflicts between rights, grapple with difficult moral and policy issues and contest misappropriations of rights;[4] in short, engage with the real world. Understanding human rights as requiring both law and politics requires a particular, and to some extent new, set of skills.

Capacity building

In chapter 2 we saw how NGOs are navigating complex relationships with governments and corporations, working with *and* against, attempting to lobby and advocate as well as engage and assist. Human rights organizations, concerned for their independence, are often wary of partnership. Yet criticism, even constructive criticism, is not enough; there are times when we need to contribute concretely to building solutions.

> 'We still need the well-practised human rights techniques – "naming and shaming", letter-writing campaigns, taking test cases, and so on... But, in addition to the classic human rights methodologies, we need new skills and techniques if we are to engage effectively in policymaking. For example, we need indicators, benchmarks and impact assessments that address [human rights]. We need to be able to analyze budgets and to identify which trade-offs are permissible and impermissible in international human rights law.' ∎
>
> Paul Hunt, UN Special Rapporteur on the Right to Health, *Essex Human Rights Review 2(1)* (2004).

The shift, in Latin America or South Africa, from authoritarian rule to greater democracy, political violence to criminal violence, from public support for human rights in the cause of the just, to public opposition when human rights are seen to defend criminals, is a case in point. Police, for example, must come to see their role as protecting human rights rather than being impeded by them: 'police reform... presents (at least) two major challenges. The first is the need to confront popular attitudes toward security and reframe a public discourse that posits a trade-off between guarantees of rights and maintaining social order... The second challenge is to offer another model of policing: specifically, concrete practices that are effective in preventing crime and enforcing laws while also respecting rights.'[5]

Adopting a meaningful human rights stance will take most NGOs beyond familiar territory and proven capacity. Skills deficits may include policymaking, understanding and promoting the full range of rights, institutional and management reform and an ability to forge new kinds of relationships with the public and state.

Testimony and narrative

In chapter 3 we looked at some alternatives to formal legal proceedings, such as truth commissions. The 1990s saw a proliferation of these and other platforms

Other ways of securing human rights

for testimony and personal narrative as a potent vehicle for advancing human rights,[6] including UN mechanisms, global conferences, national human rights institutions, 24-hour news broadcasts, the internet, a growing market for alternative autobiography (see box), and an explosion in the number and reach of NGOs and social movements.

Commodification of truth-telling for some of these 'markets' can result in an unsettling conjunction between suffering and selling. Other negative consequences may be a culture of victimhood, or loss of control by those testifying over how their story is represented, interpreted and disseminated. However, human rights narratives have the capacity to assert both universality and difference, holding the global and local in dialog. Testimony can humanize the hitherto abstract, transcend cultural and political difference, and engender solidarity among strangers. By engaging with the stories and reflecting on the lived experiences of individuals and peoples, they become part of our lives in a way that brings us to respect others.[7]

National human rights institutions

In addition to truth commissions and law courts, other state-based institutions that help to uphold rights and the rule of law include human rights commissions and ombudsmen, collectively known as national

---

'My name is Rigoberta Menchú. I am 23 years old. This is my testimony. I didn't learn it from a book and I didn't learn it alone. I'd like to stress that it's not only *my* life, it's also the testimony of my people. It's hard for me to remember everything that's happened to me in my life . . . The important thing is that what has happened to me has happened to many other people too: My story is the story of all poor Guatemalans. My personal experience is the reality of a whole people.' ■

R Menchú, *I, Rigoberta Menchú: An Indian Woman in Guatemala*, ed E Burgos-Debray (Verso 1984) p 1.

human rights institutions (NHRIs). Complementing the work of NGOs and international organizations, NHRIs are meant to be autonomous organs of the state with functions varying from human rights education, monitoring, documentation, investigation and arbitration, to acting as an *amicus curiae* ('friend of the court') in cases with human rights implications. In practice their activities range from improving the status of the isolated Tsaatan minority in Mongolia, rehabilitating former child soldiers in Uganda, re-opening decades-old cases of forced disappearance in Mexico and helping to train police in Northern Ireland, to gauging the views of ordinary Afghanis on matters of security.[8] The UN's 'Paris Principles' are the accepted international standard on how NHRIs should be established and maintained in order to protect their independence and effectiveness. Details of NHRIs around the world – numbering more than a hundred, though not all genuine – are available at: www.nhri.net

Global civil society

An emergent global civil society is a strong indicator and driver of the idea of universal human rights. Sometimes, for strategic reasons, or simply because there is no effective (or safe) domestic legal or political recourse, it is necessary for local activists to forge international connections. External pressure on an abusive state may then come directly from a partner NGO and its constituency (in the form of, say, a letter-writing campaign or consumer boycott) or may be exerted by pressuring Northern governments to bring influence to bear (see chart). Southern actors gain access, leverage, information and other resources, while Northern partners gain credibility for their solidarity claims.[9] Such activism is part of the second human rights revolution, as new actors, relationships and political struggles reshape international relations.

A model of securing human rights

Analogies incorporated in this model are: a boomerang, in which local activists seek partners abroad to exert external pressure on the offending state; a spiral, in which domestic resistance and repeated boomerang 'throws' build on prior successes; and a pincer, in which pressure is exerted from above and below, inside and without. This model could also be adapted to apply to non-state actors infringing rights. It is a simplified reflection of reality, of course; sometimes the spiral may come to a standstill and/or wind back to a state of increased violation. Getting a government in denial to make concessions is usually the biggest challenge in the spiral; retreat from concessions is the most likely setback. 'The spiral keeps spiraling only if transnational civil society makes it happen.'

Violating state	Local human rights activists	International partners
Repression/violation	• domestic opposition weak &/or persecuted • domestic activism too dangerous or ineffectual • seek international support	• receive information from domestic opposition • invoke international/regional human rights norms &/or mechanisms • mobilize NGOs, international organizations, sympathetic states & public • pressure the repressive state directly & lobby foreign states to add pressure • may help fund struggling domestic groups
Denial/backlash • denies validity of human rights • attacks credibility of claims & claimants • asserts sovereignty • may generate some domestic resentment of international interference &/or fear of instability	• domestic opposition builds • mobilize new domestic actors • may suffer renewed attacks	• maintain bilateral & multi-lateral pressure

Tactical concessions • cosmetic improvements attempt to deflect criticism • concedes validity of rights claims & engages with critics • concessions reduce the state's control over the situation & its margin of maneuver • potential for 'entrapment'	• focus of activity shifts to domestic activists (emboldened by their success & protected to some extent by their international links) • maintain links to transnational networks • invoke norms/mechanisms • impart & receive information • respond to state rhetoric with renewed evidence of violations & moral argument (engaging state in dialog increases likelihood of entrapment)		• time to use shaming techniques & negative pressure ('sticks')
Change of policy &/or regime • accepts the validity of human rights norms but practice inconsistent • ratifies international treaties • institutionalizes rights in domestic law • establishes complaint mechanisms • apologizes, compensates, etc. • human rights education for public officials	• expand into new political space • human rights enter societal discourse		• maintain pressure from above & below to ensure behavior conforms to rhetoric (new regime may retreat from rights protection once its position is consolidated)
Respect for human rights • improved practices backed by the rule of law	• rights are 'mainstreamed', internalized, 'taken for granted' • human rights culture emerges		• reduced network activity

ME Keck & K Sikkink, *Activists Beyond Borders: Advocacy Networks in International Politics* (Cornell University Press 1998) pp 12–13; T Risse, SC Ropp, K Sikkink (eds), *The Power of Human Rights: International Norms and Domestic Change* (Cambridge University Press 1999) pp 17–35; T Risse, 'The power of norms versus the norms of power: Transnational civil society and human rights' in AM Florini (ed), *The Third Force: The Rise of Transnational Civil Society* (Japan Center for International Exchange: Tokyo and Carnegie Endowment for International Peace: Washington DC 2000) p 191.

Other ways of securing human rights

Such collaborations may incur difficulties, however. In the experience of Jubilee 2000, an international coalition of civil society campaigns to cancel unpayable Third-World debt, 'Northern campaigns were almost invariably better funded and resourced, and therefore had a distinct advantage in terms of access to information, ability to implement strategy, and mobilizing and lobbying key politicians... Nearly all Southern campaigns were ultimately dependent on Northern campaigns and organizations for funding... the relationship between Northern and Southern campaigns was never an equal one... This situation led at times to tension, with Southern campaigns claiming that the North was seeking to speak on their behalf [and questioning] the "politically expedient" tactics of Northern campaigns which it felt undermined the radical and longer-term demands of Southern campaigns.'[10]

We have looked at the benefits of a principled politics and the need to exert political pressure to secure human rights, and at some newer areas of human rights activism, but what about some of the more conventional kinds of pressure? A political strategy may employ carrots or sticks, as appropriate, of a legal, political or economic nature. Here are just a few examples.

Naming, shaming and persuading

Changing attitudes and behaviors – of an individual or collective entity – is a psychological as well as political task for which there is a toolkit of persuasion techniques. Look closely at the next appeal letter you receive from an NGO seeking your money or support. In addition to convincing you of their cause and credentials, they seek to overcome your sense of powerlessness with the idea that you can 'do something' by supporting their organization. They may try to anticipate and counteract common excuses for not acting: 'No, it's not true that the problem is so enormous that a few dollars won't make a difference. No, the money won't go to bolster a corrupt regime. No, we are not hostile to this particular country.'[11] They appeal to your higher self – sense of duty, compassion or positive self-image – mounting a moral case, perhaps with emotional examples and graphic images, citing your previous record of generosity and concern, and calling for consistent behavior (your continued support). A similar approach can be taken to politicians and business leaders, appealing to their personal mores and public image, citing, where possible, past instances of praiseworthy behavior (both theirs and their peers') and the benefits of a pro-rights stance.

'Shaming' is more to the 'stick' end of the spectrum with the threat or reality of public exposure and condemnation. Most governments care about their domestic legitimacy and international standing, and most corporations rely on public image and positive associations with their 'brand'.

Economic measures

So maybe shaming hasn't worked. More tangible pressure can be brought to bear. Civil society can advocate and monitor sanctions, for example, or act directly to achieve similar effects through consumer boycotts of specific companies, products or nations. Of course, sanctions can have an egregious effect on human rights, as occurred in Iraq in the 1990s, hence the advent of 'smart' sanctions that attempt to avoid such negative effects, perhaps by targeting the travel plans and bank accounts of political leaders. Making aid, debt relief or membership of some desirable international organization conditional on human rights performance may also provide the necessary leverage, although again with potential risks to innocent parties that ought to be assessed and monitored.

Other ways of securing human rights

> 'We make the law, we use the law and, where necessary, we break the law.' ∎
>
> Paraphrasing Mark Heywood, Treatment Action Campaign, South Africa (2005).

Civil disobedience and nonviolence

Another way of exerting pressure to realize human rights may be not to uphold the law, but to break it. A long and proud tradition of nonviolent resistance takes

---

Defending the right to life

In 2003 five pacifists broke into Shannon Airport in Ireland and took to a US navy airplane with hammers (one of them inflatable). The trespassers from the Catholic Worker movement also poured human blood on the runway, painted anti-war slogans on the hangar and erected a 'shrine' to casualties of the war, including photos of dead children and copies of the Qur'an and the Bible. Ireland is allegedly neutral in the war on Iraq, but allows the US to use its airport as a 'pit stop' for military traffic to and from the war, including those ill-fated captives bound for Guantánamo Bay.

Deirdre Clancy, Nuin Dunlop, Karen Fallon, Damien Moran and Ciaron O'Reilly – 'Pit-stop Plowshares' activists inspired by the Hebrew prophecy that nations 'shall beat their swords into plowshares, and... study war no more' – were arrested and charged with criminal damage worth millions of dollars. Facing up to 10 years' jail if convicted, they claimed they were upholding rather than breaking the law, in the same way it would be legal to break down the door of a burning building to save anyone trapped inside.

The disabled plane did not proceed to Iraq, but was returned to Texas. Three private troop transport companies also pulled out of Ireland, allegedly in response to the protestors' action. Nonetheless, thousands more US military personnel have since passed through Shannon Airport, and thousands more Iraqis have been killed.

When the activists were put on trial, former US Marine Sgt Jimmy Massey admitted in the witness box to complicity in breaching the Geneva Conventions when, during a three-month tour in 2003, his platoon shot dead 30 Iraqi civilians. Since such breaches can be tried in Ireland under the *Geneva Conventions Act 1962*, the defendants claim they were acting to uphold both international and domestic law. ∎

www.peaceontrial.com; http://plowsharesactions.org; Book of Isaiah 2:4.

the moral position that obedience to an unjust power amounts to complicity in injustice.[12] Participants sometimes prepare with training in how to respond to violence, arrest or imprisonment. Others may refrain from illegal action in order to support and assist those arrested. Civil disobedience was used to effect in 20th-century struggles of colonized peoples of Asia and Africa – most famously the Indian independence movement led by Gandhi – and also the African-American human rights movement led by Martin Luther King. It is most visible today as an expression of opposition to the escalation of the US-led war on Iraq (see box).

Other nonviolent human rights activists seek alternatives to military enforcement (discussed in chapter 3). Practitioners include Peace Brigades International, whose unarmed members aim to protect at-risk human rights defenders simply by their presence,[13] and Nonviolent Peaceforce, which seeks to establish a trained, international civilian 'peaceforce' for deployment to protect human rights and deter violence.

Unintended effects and entrapment

'In the 1940s the US and Britain led efforts to replace a world of chaos and conflict with a new, rules-based system... Over the next 50 years, the mission to deepen and develop international law was, broadly speaking, successful... But it may have been too successful... The rules which were intended to constrain others became constraining of their creators. Human rights norms took on a life of their own. They came to be applied in ways which were politically inconvenient...' ■
International lawyer Philippe Sands, *Lawless World: America and the Making and Breaking of Global Rules* (Allen Lane 2005) p xi.

In this complex world, we cannot know the full impact of our activism, whether of the traditional or newer kind, nor can even the most powerful actors control all variables. Seeds sown now can produce unlikely and unexpected fruit in the future. South

Other ways of securing human rights

Africa's Truth and Reconciliation Commission, for instance, was not expected to be independent enough to criticize the ruling ANC, but it did. Similarly, some state-based human rights institutions set up to be useless find ways of being effective. Indonesian President Suharto was one who cynically established a National Commission for Human Rights that came back to bite him.

Such processes of entrapment are not necessarily random or serendipitous, however. State and non-state rights violators making minor concessions under pressure 'almost uniformly underestimate the impact of these changes, and overestimate their own support among their population. They think the changes are less costly than they are, and they anticipate that they have greater control over international and domestic processes. Leaders of authoritarian states (like many political scientists) tend to believe that "talk is cheap" and do not understand the degree to which they can become "entrapped" in their own rhetoric...'[14] Governments may sign up to treaties they have no intention of implementing; but with pressure from civil society, other states and inter-governmental organizations, they can be forced to comply. The same can be true of corporate codes of conduct, the World Bank's policy guidelines on human rights issues, such as involuntary resettlement and indigenous peoples and, indeed, NGO rhetoric about accountability.

Human rights education

The great strength of a human rights framework over other models of social justice is the empowering potential of a sense of entitlement. That sense will be lacking where people are unaware of their rights. One of the four internationally recognized aims of all education – whether public, private, formal or informal – is to strengthen respect for human rights and fundamental freedoms.[15] Human rights

'Consider two approaches. The first could be termed a "violations" [approach] and the second a "promotional" approach. The former focuses on denouncing violations of human rights and on enforcement through legal remedies. The latter emphasizes positive ways to engage governments, important non-state actors, civil society organizations, and poor, marginalized communities themselves in the pursuit of rights through education, dialogue and advocacy... both of these approaches are necessary.' ■

A Jones, 'The case of CARE International in Rwanda' in P Gready & J Ensor (eds), *Reinventing Development? Translating Rights-Based Approaches from Theory into Practice* (Zed Books 2005) p 97.

education is fundamental to the forging of human rights movements and, more generally, a 'human rights culture'.

Human rights violations are often not so much extreme and obvious as insidious. Human rights education makes the invisible visible.[16] The Howard Government in Australia appears to despise human rights, yet tolerates human rights education. Human rights education may simply mean teaching people about what rights are or, more controversially, raising awareness about which of their rights are being eroded and why. Should human rights education be inoffensive and inclusive – something even the Australian Government can support – or should it be political and divisive? The answer is not obvious. There may be merit in keeping everyone engaged in dialog about rights rather than alienated by a more adversarial stance. US philosopher Richard Rorty explores another dilemma (see box below).

Building a human rights culture

Closely related to human rights education, but with a broader agenda, is the building of a robust culture of human rights in communities of all sizes, from the local to the global – a subject much discussed in South Africa with the adoption of its new Constitution in 1996 and in the UK with the introduction of the

'Sentimental' education for a rights culture

Is respecting human rights about being moral or being nice? Rorty argues, reluctantly but pragmatically, for the effectiveness of appealing to hearts rather than minds:

'If, like many of us, you teach students who have been brought up in the shadow of the Holocaust, brought up believing that prejudice against racial or religious groups is a terrible thing, it is not very hard to convert them to standard liberal views about abortion, gay rights and the like... You do this by manipulating their sentiments in such a way that they imagine themselves in the shoes of the despised and oppressed. Such students are already so nice that they are eager to define their identity in non-exclusionary terms. The only people they have trouble being nice to are the ones they consider irrational – the religious fundamentalist, the smirking rapist, or the swaggering skinhead...

But it is not a good idea to encourage these students to label "irrational" the intolerant people they have trouble tolerating... The bad people's beliefs are not more or less "irrational" than the belief that race, religion, gender and sexual preference are all morally irrelevant... The bad people's problem is that they were not so lucky in the circumstances of their upbringing as we were... We should treat them as deprived [of] security and sympathy. By "security" I mean conditions of life sufficiently risk-free as to make one's difference from others inessential to one's self-respect, one's sense of worth... By "sympathy" I mean the sort of reaction that... we have more of after watching TV programs about the genocide in Bosnia. Security and sympathy go together... The tougher things are, the more you have to be afraid of, the more dangerous your situation, the less you can afford the time or effort to think about what things might be like for people with whom you do not immediately identify. Sentimental education only works on people who can relax long enough to listen.

...But it is revolting to think that our only hope for a decent society consists in softening the self-satisfied hearts of a leisure class... Why does this preference make us resist the thought that sentimentality may be the best weapon we have? ...We resist out of resentment. We resent the idea that we shall have to wait for the strong to turn their piggy little eyes to the suffering of the weak. We desperately hope that there is something stronger and more powerful that will hurt the strong if they do not – if not a vengeful God, then a vengeful aroused proletariat, or, at least, a vengeful superego...' ∎

R Rorty, 'Human Rights, Rationality and Sentimentality' in S Hurley & S Shute (eds), *On Human Rights: The 1993 Oxford Amnesty Lectures* (Basic Books 1993) pp 112-34.

Human Rights Act 1998. For Canadian scholar Michael Ignatieff, our goal should be nations founded not on race or ethnicity, but on 'civic nationalism' and constitutionalism: 'a community of equal, rights-bearing citizens, united in patriotic attachment to a shared set of political practices and values'.[17]

The language of human rights may already be the dominant moral vocabulary of our time, influencing a great breadth of issues and actors, both state and non-state, from development and humanitarianism to trade and foreign policy. The challenge of such 'mainstreaming' is to avoid co-option or dilution, and to ensure shared vocabulary finds expression, not only in rules and institutions, but in values, relationships and processes. Conflict management practitioners Galant and Parlevliet[18] have a multi-faceted model to describe what a human rights culture might look like:

* rights as rules (legal rights, codes of conduct, customary rights, etc)
* rights as structures and institutions (courts, commissions, policies, committees – institutionalized remedies that address underlying causes such as the division of power and resources)
* rights as relationships (vertical and horizontal relationships between groups, individuals and the state built on justice, equality and dignity)
* rights as process (processes infused with 'human rights values' – equality, justice, non-discrimination, participation, diversity, peace, etc – enhance the validity and sustainability of outcomes)

A culture of rights exists where rights are embedded – owned, understood and realized – in everyday life. It requires legislative, institutional and organizational change and vigilance as well as attitudinal and behavioral change. Where rights have a taken-for-granted quality, legal and institutional protections become a remedy of last resort.

Other ways of securing human rights

'The human rights movement is not about winning or losing. It is an open project. I can never afford to declare victory, neither can you. On the contrary, we need to renew our commitments to this struggle, and certainly we cannot announce the end of anything. If there is anything we can announce, it is just the very beginning.' ∎
– Former UN High Commissioner for Human Rights, the late Sérgio Vieira de Mello
'Five questions for the human rights field', *Sur International Journal on Human Rights (1)* (2004) pp 165-71, www.surjournal.org/eng

1 J Drèze, 'Democracy and the Right to Food' in P Alston & M Robinson (eds), *Human Rights and Development: Towards Mutual Reinforcement* (Oxford University Press 2005) pp 61-2. **2** N Stammers, 'Social movements and the social construction of human rights', *Human Rights Quarterly* 21(4) (1999) pp 996-1000. **3** P O'Brien, 'Rights-based responses to aid politicization in Afghanistan' in P Gready & J Ensor (eds), *Reinventing Development? Translating Rights-Based Approaches from Theory into Practice* (Zed Books 2005) pp 201-8. **4** P Gready, 'Politics of Human Rights,' *Third World Quarterly* 24(4) (2003) pp 745-57. **5** R Neild, 'Human rights NGOs, police and citizen security in transitional democracies,' *Journal of Human Rights 2(3)* (2003) p 290. **6** K Schaffer & S Smith, *Human Rights and Narrated Lives: The Ethics of Recognition* (Palgrave Macmillan 2004). **7** A Langlois, *The Politics of Justice and Human Rights: Southeast Asia and Universalist Theory* (Cambridge University Press 2001) p 168. **8** Office of the High Commissioner for Human Rights, 'Actors for change: The growth of human rights institutions' www.un.org **9** ME Keck & K Sikkink, *Activists Beyond Borders: Advocacy Networks in International Politics* (Cornell University Press 1998) pp 12-13. **10** N Buxton, 'Debt cancellation and civil society: A case study of Jubliee 2000' in P Gready (ed), *Fighting for Human Rights* (Routledge 2004) pp 67-8. **11** S Cohen, *States of Denial: Knowing About Atrocities and Suffering* (Polity 2001) p 199. **12** J Schell, *The Unconquerable World: Power, Nonviolence, and the Will of the People* (Metropolitan Books 2003). **13** LE Eguren & L Mahony, *Unarmed Bodyguards: International Accompaniment for the Protection of Human Rights* (Kumarian Press 1997). **14** T Risse, SC Ropp & K Sikkink (eds), *The Power of Human Rights: International Norms and Domestic Change* (Cambridge University Press 1999) p 27. **15** *Charter of the United Nations* Art. 55(c); UDHR Art. 26(2); *Convention Against Discrimination in Education* Art. 5(1)(a); ICERD Art. 7; ICESCR Art. 13(1); CRC Art. 29(1)(b); UNESCO/ILO *Recommendation Concerning the Status of Teachers* principle 1 and *Cairo Declaration on Human Rights in Islam* Article 9(b); see also CESCR *General Comment 13: The right to education (Art.13)* UN Doc. E/C.12/1999/10, para. 4. **16** A Durbach, Director of the Australian Human Rights Centre at the University of New South Wales, speaking at the Fulbright Symposium on Peace and Human Rights Education (Melbourne, 22 June 2005). **17** M Ignatieff, *Blood and Belonging: Journeys into the New Nationalism* (Vintage 1994) pp 3-4. **18** G Galant & M Parlevliet, 'Using rights to address conflict – a valuable synergy' in P Gready & J Ensor (eds), *Reinventing Development? Translating Rights-Based Approaches from Theory into Practice* (Zed Books 2005) pp 114-18.

Contacts and resources

International

Amnesty International
www.amnesty.org

Anti-Slavery International
www.antislavery.org

Disabled Peoples' International
www.dpi.org

International P.E.N./Writers in
Prison Committee
www.internationalpen.org.uk

Peace Brigades International
www.peacebrigades.org

People's Movement for Human
Rights Education
www.pdhre.org

Red Cross and Red Crescent Societies
www.ifrc.org

Survival
www.survival-international.org

UNICEF (United Nations Children's
Fund)
www.unicef.org

United Nations Associations
www.wfuna.org

WaterAid
www.wateraid.org

Africa

Centre for Conflict Resolution
http://ccrweb.ccr.uct.ac.za

Tostan ('Breakthrough')
www.tostan.org

Australia

Australians for Native Title and
Reconciliation (ANTaR)
www.antar.org.au
New Matilda
www.humanrightsact.com.au

Project Respect
www.projectrespect.org.au

Rights Australia
www.rightsaustralia.org.au

Rural Australians for Refugees
**www.ruralaustraliansforrefu-
gees.org**

Canada

Assembly of First Nations (AFN)
www.afn.ca

CUSO
www.cuso.org

Egale Canada
www.egale.ca

Equitas
www.equitas.org

John Humphrey Centre for Peace
and Human Rights
www.johnhumphreycentre.org

KAIROS Canadian Ecumenical
Justice Initiatives
www.kairoscanada.org

Mining Watch Canada
www.miningwatch.ca

Europe

Advice on Individual Rights in
Europe (AIRE)
www.airecentre.org/about_us.html

Contacts and resources

Centre on Housing Rights and
Evictions
www.cohre.org

European Council on Refugees &
Exiles
www.ecre.org
International Council on Human
Rights Policy
www.ichrp.org

UK

Action Aid
www.actionaid.org

Article 19
promotes freedom of expression
and freedom of information
www.article19.org

Bail for Immigration Detainees (BID)
www.biduk.org

British Institute of Human Rights
www.bihr.org

British-Irish Rights Watch
www.birw.org

Campaign Against Arms Trade (CAAT)
www.caat.org.uk

Global Witness
www.globalwitness.org

Interights
www.interights.org

Jubilee Debt Campaign
www.jubileedebtcampaign.org.uk

Kurdish Human Rights Project
(KHRP)
www.khrp.org

Landmine Action
www.landmineaction.org

Liberty
www.liberty-human-rights.org.uk

Medical Foundation for the Care of
Victims of Torture
www.torturecare.org.uk

Minority Rights Group (MRG)
www.minorityrights.org
Penal Reform International (PRI)
www.penalreform.org

Redress
www.redress.org

Womenaid International
www.womenaid.org

US

Human Rights Watch
www.hrw.org

Derechos Human Rights
www.derechos.net

Americas

Center for Legal and Social Studies
www.cels.org.ar/

Fighting Against Forced
Disappearances in Latin America
(FEDEFAM)
**www.desaparecidos.org/
fedefam/eng.html**

Mothers of the Plaza de Mayo
www.madres.org/

Landless Workers Movement of
Brazil
www.mstbrazil.org/

Partnership Africa Canada
www.pacweb.org/

Rigoberta Menchu Foundation
http://www.rigobertamenchu.org/
Asia Pacific

Asia Human Rights Commission
www.ahrchk.net/

Asia Pacific Human Rights Network
www.aphrn.org/

Asian Forum for Human Rights and
Development
www.forum-asia.org/

Commonwealth Human Rights
Initiative
www.humanrightsinitiative.org

Human Rights Commission of
Pakistan
www.hrcp-web.org

International Women's Rights Action
Watch- Asia Pacific (IWRAW- AP)
www.iwraw-ap.org/

New Matilda
www.humanrightsact.com.au

Odhikar
www.odhikar.org/

Middle East

Arab Institute for Human Rights
www.aihr.org.tn

Al-Mezan Center for Human Rights
www.mezan.org/

B'Tselem – The Israeli Information
Center for Human Rights in the
Occupied Territories
www.btselem.org/index.asp

Egyptian Organization for Human
Rights
www.eohr.org/

Palestinian Center for Human
Rights
www.pchrgaza.org/

Arab Commission for Human Rights
www.achr.nu/achr.en.htm

The Arabic Network for Human
Rights Information
www.hrinfo.net/en/

Bibliography

Amnesty International annual reports
www.amnesty.org/ailib/aireport/index.html

Amnesty Oxford Lecture Series
www.oxford-amnesty-lectures.org

U Baxi, *The Future of Human Rights* (Oxford University Press: New York 2006)

D Buss & A Manji (eds) *International Law: Modern Feminist Approaches* (Hart: Oxford 2005)

J Cowan, M-B Dembour & R Wilson (eds) *Culture and Rights: Anthropological Perspectives* (Cambridge University Press: Cambridge 2001)

T Dunne & N Wheeler (eds) *Human Rights in Global Politics* (Cambridge University Press: Cambridge 1999)

LE Eguren & L Mahony, *Unarmed Bodyguards: International Accompaniment for the Protection of Human Rights* (Kumarian Press: Bloomfield, Connecticut 1997)

W Felice, *The Global New Deal: Economic and Social Human Rights in World Politics* (Rowman & Littlefield: Lanham, Maryland 2003)

D Forsythe, *Human Rights in International Relations*, 2nd edn (Cambridge University Press: Cambridge 2006)

M Freeman, *Human Rights: An Interdisciplinary Approach* (Polity: Cambridge 2002)

MA Glendon, *A World Made New: Eleanor Roosevelt and the Universal Declaration of Human Rights* (Random House: New York 2001)

P Gready (ed.) *Fighting for Human Rights* (Routledge: London 2004)

P Gready & J Ensor (eds) *Reinventing Development? Translating Rights-Based Approaches from Theory into Practice* (Zed Books: London 2005)

H Hannum, *Guide to International Human Rights Practice*, 3rd edn (Transnational: Ardsley, NY 1999)

P Hayner, *Unspeakable Truths: Confronting State Terror and Atrocity – How Truth Commissions around the World are Challenging the Past and Shaping the Future* (Routledge: New York 2001)

Human Rights Watch World Reports
www.hrw.org/doc/?t=pubs

International Council on Human Rights Policy publications
www.ichrp.org/public/publications.php?lang=AN

MR Ishay, *The History of Human Rights: From Ancient Times to the Globalization Era* (University of California Press: Berkeley 2004)

M Keck & K Sikkink, *Activists Beyond Borders: Advocacy Networks in International Politics* (Cornell University Press: Ithaca 1998)

J Mann, S Gruskin, M Grodin & G Annas (eds) *Health and Human Rights: A Reader* (Routledge: New York 1999)

S Marks & A Clapham *International Human Rights Lexicon* (Oxford University Press: Oxford 2005)

P Sands, *Lawless World: America and the Making and Breaking of Global Rules* (Allen Lane: Melbourne 2005)

J Schell, *The Unconquerable World: Power, Nonviolence, and the Will of the People* (Metropolitan Books: New York 2003)

A Sen, *Development as Freedom* (Oxford University Press: Oxford 2001)

RKM Smith & C van den Anker, *The Essentials of Human Rights: Everything You Need to Know about Human Rights* (Hodder Arnold: London 2005)

HJ Steiner & P Alston, *International Human Rights in Context: Law, Politics, Morals* (Oxford University Press: Oxford 2000)

P Uvin, *Human Rights and Development* (Kumarian Press: Bloomfield, Connecticut 2004)

Index

Index

Index

Index

Index

Index

Index